BABY
NAMES

BABY NAMES

over
2000
new and
traditional boys'
and girls' names

Bounty Books

First published in Great Britain in 2001 by
Chancellor Press, an imprint of Bounty Books

This edition published 2005 by Bounty Books,
a division of Octopus Publishing Group Ltd
2–4 Heron Quays, London E14 4JP

ISBN 0 7537 1225 3
ISBN13 9780753712252

A CIP catalogue record for this book is available
from the British Library

Printed and bound in Great Britain

CONTENTS

Boys'
Names

AARON (Aron)
A Biblical name believed to be of Egyptian origin.
Among the top fifty in the United States, Canada
and Australia, it is gaining ground in Britain.

ABE see **ABRAHAM**

ABEL
Possibly derived from the Hebrew word for 'breath' or
'son'. The second son of Adam and Eve, a shepherd,
murdered in a fit of jealousy by his brother Cain.

ABRAHAM (Abe, Abram)
From the Hebrew word for 'eternal father of the multi-
tudes'. The name of the first patriarch and father of the
Hebrews was originally **Abram**, the favoured British
form until after the Reformation.

ADAM
Stems from the Hebrew for 'red', from the red earth.
The name of the first man, it is one of the oldest in
existence.

ADRIAN
Means, 'dark riches'. From the Latin name Adrianus,
describing a man from the town of Adria.

AIDAN
An ancient Irish name from a word meaning 'little fiery
one'. St Aidan was a 7th-century monk who founded a
monastery on Lindisfarne, where English boys were
educated.

AIKEN
Means, 'made of oak'. An Old English name that has a second meaning in the North of England – 'little Adam', implying that the baby is the image of his father.

AINSLEY (Ainslie)
Originally a surname, meaning 'my meadow', which has become a popular first name.

ALAN (Allan, Allen, Allin, Alyn, Alun)
Originally a Celtic name meaning 'harmony', the name of an early Welsh and Breton saint. The name may also have a Gaelic origin, meaning 'handsome' or 'rock-solid'.

ALARIC
From the Old German meaning 'ruler of all'. The Visigoth King, Alaric I, was responsible for the sacking of Rome in AD 410. The Victorians revived the name in the mid-19th century.

ALASTAIR (Alistair, Alasdair)
The Scottish form of **Alexander**, meaning 'man's defender'.

ALBAN
From the Latin meaning 'white'. St Alban was the first British martyr. A Romano-Briton, he lived in Verulamium, now the city of St Albans.

ALBERT (Al, Bert, Bertie, Halbert)
From the Old German Adalbert, meaning 'noble' and 'bright', or 'illustrious'.

ALDOUS
Derived from the Latinised version of the Old German word meaning 'old'.

ALEC
A shortened form of **Alexander** used as a name in its own right.

ALEXANDER (Alec, Alex, Alick, Alistair, Alix, Sandy)
From the Greek meaning 'defender of men'. Bestowed apon many saints, martyrs and kings, it has been a popular name for over three thousand years.

ALFRED (Al, Alf, Alfie, Fred)
Means 'elf-counsel' in Anglo-Saxon; in early English history elves were regarded as powerful spirits of nature. Also means 'wise advice'.

ALGERNON
A French name, meaning 'with a moustache'. Supposedly a nickname given to an 11th-century Count of Boulogne, named **Eustace**, to avoid confusion with his father who had the same name.

ALISTAIR (Alastair, Alister, Alisdair)
The phonetic spelling of Alasdair and the Gaelic version of **Alexander**.

ALPHONSE (Alfie, Alfons)
Means 'ready for battle'.

ALUN see **ALAN**

ALVIN
From the German meaning 'noble friend'. Possibly an updated version of the Old English name Alwyn.

AMADEUS
Means 'lovable'.

AMBROSE (Emrys)
From the Greek, meaning 'pertaining to the Immortals'. Ambrosia was the food of the Gods, as nectar was their drink.

AMOS
Means 'worried' in Hebrew and was the name of one of the Old Testament prophets.

ANATOLE
Literally means 'rising sun'. This is the Greek name for the main part of Turkey, and a meeting place for traders between the East and West in ancient times.

ANDREW (Anderson, Andie, Andreas, Andy, Drew)
Comes from the Greek meaning 'manly' and was the name of the first apostle.

ANEURIN
From the Welsh meaning 'gold'. The Welsh Labour politician, Aneurin Bevan (1897-1960) made this famous in modern times.

ANGUS
From the Gaelic word meaning 'unique choice'. Originally a Scottish name, Aonghus. The Scottish clan

MacDonell have used the name Angus since the
15th century.

ANTHONY (Anton, Antony, Tony)
From a Roman family name which means both 'price-
less' and 'flourishing'. Many saints have this name,
including St Anthony of Egypt (251-356), and St
Anthony of Padua (1195-1231), a famous preacher
and patron of lost property.

ARCHIBALD (Archie)
Derived from an Old German word meaning 'truly
bold'. Another of the names brought to England by the
Norman Conquest. The clans Campbell and Douglas
particularly favour this name.

ARNOLD (Arn, Arny)
From the Old German Arenvald meaning 'eagle power'.
This modern name is probably a later development
from the Latin form Arnoldus. It was rare until the
1870s; revived in honour of Thomas Arnold, reforming
headmaster of Rugby.

ARTHUR (Art)
An old name of uncertain roots. It is probably of Latin
origin, as there was a Roman family name Artorius,
though it could be from the Celtic *artos*, 'a bear', or
Irish *art*, 'a stone'. The name may also refer to the
Norse god of war, Thor.

ASA
From the Hebrew meaning 'healer' or 'physician'.

ASHLEY (Ashleigh)
From the Anglo-Saxon meaning 'ash field'. Originally a place and surname, it may have been used as a first name in honour of Anthony Ashley Cooper, Earl of Shaftesbury (1801-85), the social reformer.

ASTLEY
From the Old English, meaning 'eastern wood'. Originally a place name and the family name of the barons of Hastings.

AUBREY
From the Old German word meaning 'clever ruler'. It was brought from Normandy to Britain by the de Veres, who became earls of Oxford.

AUGUSTINE
A Latin diminutive meaning 'venerable'.

AUGUSTUS (Augustine, Austin, Gus)
Means 'worthy of honour'. This esteemed title was awarded by the first Roman Emperor, Octavius Caesar, to himself.

AUSTIN (Austen, Austyn, Awstin, Ostin)
From **Augustine**, the Latin diminutive form of **Augustus**, meaning 'venerable' and 'worthy of honour'.

BALDWIN
A German-originated name meaning 'bold friend'. A
Welsh form also exists, Maldwyn.

BARNABAS
From the Aramaic, meaning 'son of consolation'. In the
New Testament, Barnabas was a companion to St Paul
and urged St Mark to write his gospel.

BARNABY (Barn, Barnabas, Barney, Barnie)
The modern version of **Barnabas**, from the Hebrew
meaning 'son of consolation'.

BARNUM
Means 'barley store'.

BARON
Means 'warrior'. The ancient feudal title for a king's
tenant is now the lowest rank of British nobility, as
well as a first name.

BARRINGTON
A common English place name and aristocratic
surname, now often used as a first name.

BARRY (Barnard, Barrie, Barrymore)
Comes from an Irish word meaning 'spear'.

**BARTHOLOMEW (Bart, Bartley, Barty, Bartle,
Batty, Tolly)**
Derived from the Hebrew meaning 'son of the furrow',
probably a name originally given to a ploughman.

BASIL (Bas, Basie)
Comes from the Greek word meaning 'kingly'. Always a very popular name in Eastern Europe, the Crusaders brought it back with them to England.

BEAU
Means 'handsome' or 'beautiful' in French.

BEAUMONT
French for 'beautiful mountain'.

BEDE
Old English for 'prayer'. An English historian, the venerable Bede (*c* 673-735) was a monk in a monastery at Jarrow.

BEN see BENJAMIN
The common abbreviation of **Benjamin** and of **Benedict,** also occurring as a name in its own right. It means 'peak' or 'mountain' and also means 'son' in Hebrew.

BENEDICT (Ben, Benedick, Benett, Bennet, Benny)
From the Latin *benedictus*, meaning 'blessed'.

BENJAMIN (Ben, Benjie, Benjy, Benny)
Comes from the Hebrew meaning 'son of the right hand'. The right hand was traditionally linked with strength.

BENTLEY
Means 'field of coarse grass'.

BERKELEY
An English place name and surname, meaning 'birch wood', now used as a first name.

BERNARD (Barnadin, Barney, Bernhard, Bjorn)
Comes from two Old German words meaning 'bear' and 'stern' or 'brave'.

BERTIE
A pet form of the names **Albert** and **Bertram**, now used independently.

BERTRAM (Bert, Bertie)
Comes from the Old German for 'bright raven'. There is also a French version, Bertrand, meaning 'bright shield'. The names became merged because of the similar sound.

BEVIS
A French name meaning 'beautiful son'.

BLAIR
The Scottish place name is a Celtic word implying a suitable place for a battle.

BLAISE
From the Latin meaning 'stuttering'. Little is known about St Blaise, a bishop martyred in the 4th century, whose feast day is the 3rd February.

BLAKE
An Anglo-Saxon name meaning 'black' or 'dark-skinned'. A place name and surname, now used as a first name.

15

BLAZE
Means 'flaming fire'. A name implying dynamism and energy.

BOAZ
From the Hebrew, meaning 'in him is strength'. In the Old Testament Ruth married the wealthy Boaz. The name was popular with Puritans in the 17th century.

BORIS
A Russian name that means 'fight'.

BOYD
Comes from the Celtic for 'yellow', probably describing the colour of hair.

BRADLEY (Brad, Braden, Brady)
Of Anglo-Saxon origin, meaning 'broad meadow'.

BRAMWELL
An Old English place name, meaning 'bramble well', and surname, now used as a first name.

BRENDAN (Brandon, Brendon)
From the Irish *Brenaian*, believed to mean 'dweller by the beacon', a more credible and certainly preferable interpretation than 'stinking hair', the meaning given by some authorities.

BRENT
A name meaning 'high'.

BRETT (Breton, Britton)
Originally a surname from the Latin meaning 'a

Breton'. Breton was the Celtic word for the people
of North-West France and their form of the Celtic
language.

BRIAN (Briant, Briar, Brien, Bryan, Byron)
An old Celtic name which may mean 'hill' or 'strength'
and has always been widespread in Ireland because of
the hero-king Brian Boru. Its use faded out quite early
but came back into fashion during the 20th century.

BRICE
Means 'son of the powerful ruler'. The name of a 5th-
century French saint much-loved in medieval Britain,
especially Scotland.

BRINDLEY
Means 'burning wood'. The place name, associated with
a woodland clearing and also with the reddish-brown
colour of wood, was used as a first name from the late
19th century, but is uncommon now.

BROCK
Means 'badger'. The Old English surname, turned first
name, is also the traditional name for a badger in folk
and children's stories, as **Bruno** is for bear.

BRODERICK
From the Norse, meaning 'brother'. It was traditionally
given to a second son.

BROOK
Means 'reward' or 'pleasure'. An Old English word
adopted as a surname before it became a first name
for both sexes.

BRUCE

Originally from a French place name Braose, now
Brieuse, probably meaning 'brushwood thicket'. It came
to Britain as a surname with the Norman Conquest.
Scottish parents began using it as a given name less
than 100 years ago and its popularity spread.

BRUNO (Brewis, Bronson, Browse)

Means 'brown' or 'bear-like'. A German name which
is also the folk name for a bear, as **Brock** is for badger.

BRUTUS

Means 'heavy' or 'unreasonable'. The name of the
Roman soldier and statesman who helped assassinate
Julius Caesar, and was immortalised in Shakespeare's
Julius Caesar.

BRYN

Stems from the Welsh word for 'hill' and has only been
used as a first name, mainly by Welsh parents, in recent
years.

BUCHAN

A Scottish place name, meaning 'little hut', and
surname, now used as a first name. It is a surname
of the barons of Tweedsmuir.

BYRON

From the Old English, meaning 'at the cattlesheds'.

C

CALEB (Cal)
From the Hebrew, meaning 'bold'. In the Old
Testament Caleb set out with Moses from Egypt and
was, with Joshua, one of the two original migrants to
enter the Promised Land.

CALLUM (Calum)
The Gaelic form of the name Columba, meaning
'dove'. St Columba left Ireland with twelve companions
to found a monastery on the island of Iona, off the West
Coast of Scotland.

CALVERT
From the Old English, meaning 'calf herder'. An
English surname, now used as a first name. It was very
popular in Victorian times.

CALVIN
Comes from the Latin for 'bald' and has been used as a
boys' name since the time of the 16th-century religious
reformer of that name.

CAMERON
Means 'crooked nose' in Gaelic. Following the recent
fashion of borrowed surnames, this Scottish clan name
is becoming very popular as a Christian name in
Scotland, Canada and Australia.

CAMPBELL
Derives from the Gaelic meaning 'crooked mouth' and
was used only as a surname until the early 20th century
when Scottish parents in particular adopted it as a fore-

name. It is not used to a great extent in the rest of
Britain, but is favoured especially in Scotland, Canada
and Australia.

CARADOC
Means 'friendly'. This popular Welsh name, from
Caradawg, honours their 1st-century hero who repelled
the Romans and after whom Cardigan is named. The
Irish form is Carthac.

CARL (Karl, Karle)
Means 'free man' or 'farmer' and is the German form of
Charles. In the United States and increasingly in Britain
Carl, with the anglicised 'c', is often used in preference
to the English **Charles**.

CARLO , CARLOS
The Italian and Spanish equivalents of **Charles**.

CARY (Carey)
The origins of this name seem uncertain. It may be
from an English place name Carew meaning 'fort',
or Welsh 'dweller in a castle', or as one authority
suggests, from the Latin 'dear'. This is a surname which
has occasionally been adopted in recent times as a
Christian name. It also occasionally occurs as a girls'
name, especially in Scotland.

CASEY
Means 'watchful' or 'brave', and can be used for both
boys and girls. It was promoted by the heroism of train
engineer Casey Jones (1864-1900), who saved many
lives after the Cannon Ball Express accident.

CASPER
Means 'imperial' or 'precious'. The English form of this German name is **Jasper**.

CASSIUS
Means 'man's defender' and is a Roman form of the Greek name. It is also a form of **Alexander**.

CECIL (Cecile, Ces)
Means 'blind' and is derived from a family name of Ancient Rome. The name of the son of Vulcan, the Roman god of fire and craftsmanship, was at first given to both sexes in the Middle Ages, then revived for boys in the 19th century.

CEDRIC
Means 'generous' or 'friendly'. It has a Victorian air about it, but its meanings and origins are unclear.

CHAD
Means 'battle' or 'warrior' and was the name of the 7th-century British saint Ceadda, noted for his humility. The name was revived in the second half of the 19th century but has always been rare.

CHARLES (Charlie, Charley, Chas, Carl, Karl, Chay)
Comes from the Old German word meaning 'a man' and has been a favourite royal name since it was adopted by the House of Stuart in the 17th century.

CHARLTON
Originally an English place name, meaning 'settlement of peasants', and a surname.

CHAS see **CHARLES**

CHAY
Strictly speaking is a short form of **Charles**, however it has also come into use as an individual name. The fame of lone yachtsman Chay Blyth, has helped to make it better known.

CHESTER
Means 'fortified castle' or 'town'. This place name has become more popular as a first name in the United States than in Britain.

CHRISTIAN (Christien, Krispin, Kristian, Chris, Kris, Kit)
Comes from the Latin *christianus*, 'a Christian'. Since the 15th century it has been a name of the Danish royal line. It has never been widely used in Britain until recently, when it has begun to come into fashion.

CHRISTOPHER (Chris)
From the Greek, meaning 'one who carries Christ'. The legendary St Christopher carried the infant Jesus across a ford. A church was built in his honour as early as 450 AD. He is the patron saint of all travellers.

CHUCK
Means 'free man' or 'farmer'. It is a popular American form of **Charles**.

CLARENCE
From the Latin meaning, 'of Clare'. Edward III created the title Duke of Clarence for his son Lionel on his marriage to a young lady of the de Clare family in 1362.

22

CLARK
Means 'clerk' or 'cleric' and was the original name for the church scholars who were the only people who could read and write. This surname has been adopted as a Christian name in the present century.

CLAUDE
From the Latin, meaning 'lame'. It came into use in Britain in the 19th century.

CLAUDIUS (Claudian, Claudio, Claus)
Means 'lame'. The Roman emperor and historian, who walked with a limp, encouraged the name's use in Roman Britain, to be revived by the Tudors in its French form, **Claudian, Claudio, Claus**.

CLAUS see NICHOLAS.

CLAYTON
Means 'clay town'. The place name, referring to local clay-pits or clay-beds, became a popular first name in the 19th century.

CLEMENT
Means 'gentle'. A name made popular first by 14 popes, and more recently the British Labour Prime Minister Clement Attlee (1883-1967).

CLIFF
An abbreviation of **Clifford** or Clifton. It has become increasingly popular in recent years as an independent name.

CLIFFORD

Derives from a place name meaning 'ford at a slope'. It became a surname and was first used as a forename in the 19th century.

CLINTON (Clint)

Comes from the Anglo-Saxon word meaning 'headland farm'. This is another surname occasionally used as a Christian name, especially in its abbreviated form, **Clint**.

CLIVE (Clifford, Clinton)

Stems from a place name meaning 'cliff' or 'steep hill', which later became a surname.

CLYDE

The name of a Scottish river, it was adopted as a Christian name early in this century, when it was quite popular in the United States. At present it reflects the rising fashion in the use of surnames.

COLE (Colier, Collis, Colvin)

Means 'coal'. A name derived from various mining place names, it has remained popular in the 20th century.

COLIN (Colan)

A French diminutive of **Nicholas** and also Celtic for 'a young hound'. It has been known since the 13th century, and is the basis of several surnames.

CONAN

Comes from the Old Celtic meaning 'high' and is best known in Ireland, though its use spread in the late 19th century through the fame of Sir Arthur Conan Doyle, creator of Sherlock Holmes.

CONNOR

A favourite Irish name, made popular by many heroes in Irish legend.

CONRAD (Conroy, Kurt)

Has its origins in the Old German word meaning 'brave counsel'. Though it was the name of a 10th-century saint it was seldom used in Britain before the mid-19th century.

CONSTANTINE

From the Latin, meaning 'constant'. Constantine the Great was the first Christian Emperor of Rome. He built the city of Constantinople on the site of ancient Byzantium, now called Istanbul.

COREY

An Irish surname, now used as a first name.

CORNELIUS (Cornel)

It is derived from a family name of Ancient Rome, and is occasionally used today.

COSMO (Cosimo)

Means 'harmony' or 'universe'. A Greek name which was adopted by the powerful Medici family of Florence, it was introduced to Scotland by the 2nd Duke of Gordon who gave it to his son.

COURTENAY (Courtney)
An aristocratic surname, now used as a first name for both boys and girls.

CRAIG
Originally a surname, stemming from the Gaelic for 'crag' it only became a forename in recent years, quickly becoming a favourite.

CRAWFORD
A Scottish place name, meaning 'ford where the crows gather', and a surname, now used as a first name.

CRISPIN
Derived from the Latin *crispus*, 'curled', it was made famous by the 3rd-century patron saint of shoemakers. It had faded out of use by the 19th century but has caught the imagination of parents in recent times.

CURTIS
Comes from the Old French word 'courteous' and is a surname which has often been used as a first name. The old spelling was Curteis.

CYRIL (Cy, Cyriack, Cyrill)
Comes from the Greek word meaning 'lord'. It was at its most popular in the 1920s, but has now gone out of fashion.

CYRUS
Comes from the Persian *kuru*, 'throne'. The Puritans adopted this name which occurs in the Old Testament and it has been a favourite in the United States, but seldom appears in Britain.

DACRE
A Cumberland place name, meaning 'trickling stream', and an aristocratic surname, now used as a first name.

DAI
The Welsh pet form of **David**.

Dale (Dallas, Dalton, Dayle)
Means 'valley'. A common surname, it has now been adopted as a Christian name for both sexes, but is usually regarded as a male name.

DAMIAN (Damien, Damion, Damon)
Comes from the Greek word meaning 'one who tames'. It was the name of the 5th-century patron saint of doctors but has only been popular with parents over the past 30 years or so.

DAMON see **DAMIAN**

DAN see **DANIEL**
An abbreviation of Daniel, but also accepted as an independent name, especially in the United States and Canada.

DANIEL (Dan, Danny)
Comes from the Hebrew meaning 'God is my judge'. It is well known through the Biblical prophet who was thrown into the lion's den, and has become increasingly fashionable since the 1950s.

DARCY
Comes from a surname, D'Arcy, which in turn came from a French place name, brought to England with the Norman Conquest. Darcy was originally used as a first name by Irish parents and its use spread to Britain.

DARELL (Darel, Darol, Darry)
Means, 'special' or 'beloved'. This surname turned first name has been fashionable since the 1940s, helped by film producer Darryl Zanuck who founded Twentieth Century Fox.

DARREN (Darrin, Darran, Darryn, Darien)
A surname meaning 'dearly beloved', first used as a given name in the United States. British parents took a great liking to it, and it has been very fashionable over the past 20 years.

DARRYL (Daryl, Darrell, Darrel, Darrol)
Comes from an Anglo-Saxon word meaning 'beloved', and was in vogue earlier this century in its various forms.

DAVID (Davy, Davey, Dai, Taffy)
Means 'darling', and comes from the Hebrew word 'beloved'. In the Bible it was the name of the boy who killed the giant Goliath and later became king of Israel, and father of the great King Solomon. The 6th century patron saint of Wales and two Scottish kings were called David, so it was always a popular name with Welsh and Scottish parents. Over the past 100 years it has been one of the top favourites all over Britain.

DEAN (Dino)
Originally a surname meaning 'valley', which stemmed
from the Anglo-Saxon. It only gained popularity as a
first name this century.

DECLAN
An ancient Gaelic name. Declan was an associate of
St Colman of Lindisfarne in the 7th century, although
little else is known about him. This name has become
hugely popular in recent years.

DENIS (Denny, Dennis)
Came originally from the Greek name Dionysos, the
god of wine and revelry, and was used in the Middle
Ages when it led to surnames such as Dennis, Dennison,
Denny and Tennyson. It was particularly popular in the
early 20th century, often spelt as **Dennis**.

DENZIL (Denzel, Denziel, Denzyl)
Originally a Cornish place name, Denzell, then a
surname, then a given name. Denzil is the usual
spelling, though there are variations such as **Denzel**
and **Denziel**. Popular in the last century, the name
has enjoyed a revival in recent years.

DEREK (Derrick, Deryk, Deryk, Rick, Ricky)
Comes from the Old German word meaning 'ruler
of the people'. A popular medieval name, revived this
century, to reach its height of popularity in the 1930s.

DERMOT
The English version of a Celtic name meaning 'free
from envy'. The 12th century king of Leister was
called Dermot so it has always been well known in

Ireland and is very popular with Irish parents today. Dairmid is the Gaelic version.

DESMOND (Des)

An Irish name meaning 'South Muster'. This was a surname adopted as a Christian name in Ireland in the 19th century and later during the century in England too. It was mildly popular in the 20th century, and is still in regular use.

DICK see RICHARD

The most usual abbreviation of **Richard**, occasionally treated as an independent name.

DICKON

A pet name for **Richard** dating back to the 13th century. Dickon was an animal loving boy in the children's classic, *The Secret Garden*, first published in 1911.

DIGBY

An English place name, meaning 'a settlement by a ditch', and a surname, used as a first name since the late 1800s.

DION

Originally the short form of Dionysos, the Greek god of wine, which also turned into **Denis**. It is popular with families of West Indian origin.

DIRK see DEREK

The Dutch form of **Derek**, sometimes adopted in English-speaking countries.

DOMINIC (Dominick, Domenic, Dom, Don, Dominique)
Stems from the Latin word meaning 'belonging to the Lord'. It has been used by Roman Catholic families since the 13th-century saint founded the Dominican order of friars. Recently it has become far more popular.

DONALD (Don, Donal, Donahue, Donovan)
Comes from the Gaelic meaning 'world-ruler' and six Scottish kings were called Donald. It has always been a favourite Highland name but has become popular with English parents.

DONOVAN
From an Irish surname, meaning 'dark brown', now popular as a first name.

DORAN
There are two meanings possible for this name: from the Greek, meaning 'gift'; or from an Irish surname, meaning 'descendant of the exile'.

DORIAN
From the Greek, meaning 'a man from Doris', which is a place in central Greece.

DOUGAL (Doughal, Dhugal)
Originally the Irish name for the Danes, from the Gaelic meaning, 'dark stranger'. It became a surname and was later taken up by Scottish parents as a first name.

DOUGLAS (Doug, Dougie)

Derives from a Celtic place name taken from the Gaelic word meaning, 'dark water', and became the surname of an important aristocratic Scottish family. By the 17th century it was used as a first name for both girls and boys. Now used only for boys, it was very popular in the middle of the 20th century.

DRAKE

Means 'serpent' or 'dragon'. A snake name associated with the Greek mythology of many countries, symbolising wisdom and immortality.

DREW

Comes from the Old French for 'sturdy' as well as being the pet name for **Andrew**. Its use as a forename in its own right is fairly new.

DUANE (Dwane, Dwayne)

Began as a Celtic surname meaning 'black', later used as a first name.

DUDLEY

Means 'Duda's clearing'. A surname that first became distinguished in Tudor times. In the 19th century it came into general use as a Christian name and still occurs periodically.

DUFF

Means 'dove', symbolising peace and love.

DUKE

Means 'leader' or 'guide', sometimes given as the shortened form of Marmaduke.

DUNCAN
Means 'dark warrior'. It has remained most popular in Scotland and is the name of the Scottish king murdered by his cousin and featured in Shakespeare's *Macbeth*.

DUNSTAN (Dunn, Dusty)
Means 'stoney hill'. It was the name of the 10th-century English saint who was Archbishop of Canterbury.

DWIGHT
This surname, originally an English derivation from the French name Diot, was adopted as a Christian name during the 19th century in the United States where it has remained in general use.

DYLAN
This is the name of a legendary Welsh hero, the son of a sea-god and means 'son of the wave'. Its popularity has increased due to the singer and songwriter Bob Dylan and the Welsh poet Dylan Thomas.

E

EAMON (Eamonn)
Means 'fortunate protector'. This Irish form of
Edmund was the name of the Irish President Eamon
de Valera (1882-1975).

EARL (Erle, Earle)
Means 'warrior' or 'chief'. It comes from the British
title and is probably more popular in the United States
than it is in Britain.

EDEN
From the Hebrew meaning 'delight'. The name of
the Biblical paradise, the country and garden in which
Adam and Eve dwelt.

EDGAR (Ed, Eddie)
From the Old English meaning 'prosperous spear' and
was the name of the first publicly acknowledged King
of England. It came into fashion in the 19th century,
then faded out of use again.

EDMUND (Edmond, Ed, Ellie, Ned, Ted, Teddie)
Derived from two Old English words meaning 'happy'
and 'protection'. It was made famous by two saints and
two early kings of England, and has never fallen out of
use. **Edmond** is a popular modern variation and the
Irish forms **Eamon** or **Eamonn** have always been well
used.

EDRIC
From the Old English, meaning 'happy ruler'. A popular
Anglo-Saxon name revived by the Victorians.

EDWARD (Ed, Eddie, Ned, Neddie, Ted, Teddy)
Edward, like **Edmund**, comes from the Old English words meaning 'happy' and 'protection', and parents have always preferred Edward. Edward has also been a recurrent name in the English royal line.

EDWIN (Ed, Edwyn, Eddie)
Stems from Old English meaning, 'rich friend' and was a common name in the days before the Norman Conquest. It became fashionable again in Victorian times. It is sometimes used as **Edwyn** and can be shortened to **Ed** or **Eddie**. Edwina is the feminine version which has remained in use.

ELDRED
From the Old English, meaning 'old counsel'. An Anglo-Saxon Christian name, one of many revived by the Victorians.

ELI
Comes from the Hebrew word for 'height'. The Puritans brought it into use in the 17th century and some families still favour it, though it is not commonly used.

ELLERY (Ellerie)
A surname, now used as a first name by both girls and boys.

ELLIOT (Eliot, Eliott)
A diminutive form of **Ellis**, from the Hebrew name Elias. A common surname, it has been taken over as a Christian name in recent years.

ELLIS

Ellis is the Old French form of the Hebrew name Elias. This is not a modern adaptation of a surname as might appear, but a form of the Biblical name. It is still used as a Christian name, especially in the United States.

ELMER

Elmer is from an Anglo-Saxon word meaning 'noble or famous'. In the United States it was especially popular at the end of the 19th century, and though still in use there, it is seldom encountered in Britain.

ELROY

A French name taken from the Latin word meaning 'regal'. A name plainly derived from the title 'the king', it is more common in the United States than in Britain.

ELTON

An Old English place name meaning 'Ella's enclosure'. It has been used as a first name only in modern times, given a boost in popularity by the singer Elton John.

ELVIS

Means 'clever friend'. An American name possibly adapted from Elvin, or from the trade name for cars, Alvis. Made fashionable by the rock-and-roll star Elvis Presley (1935-77).

ELWIN

From the Anglo-Saxon, meaning 'old friend'. A surname now used as a first name.

EMANUEL (Emmanuel, Imanuel, Manny, Manuel)
Means 'God is here'. The biblical name for Christ is a popular Jewish name. Among non-Jews it was found in Cornwall before spreading into general use last century.

EMERY
Means 'power'. The anglicised form of the German name Emmerich was given to both sexes until confined to boys in the last century.

EMLYN
From a Welsh place name, now used as a first name.

ENOCH
Means 'dedicated'. The name of Cain's son in the Bible, it was favoured by the Puritans and boosted by Tennyson's tragic poem *Enoch Arden* (1864). It is now found mostly in the North and Midlands.

ERIC
Possibly comes from Old Norse meaning 'ever ruling' or 'island ruler'. It is an ancient name in Scandinavian countries. It seems to have been brought to England by the Danes – there is an Iricus mentioned in Domesday – but no further evidence exists until the 19th century, when it appeared in the literature of the time.

ERNEST
The anglicised form of the German name Ernst, meaning 'vigour'. Ernestine is the feminine form.

ERROL

Means 'chief' or 'warrior'. Believed to be a corruption of the title 'earl'. This German form of **Earl** may also be derived from a Scottish place name. The name is by no means common in Britain, and it is more widely used in the United States.

ESMOND

From the Old English meaning 'divine protection'. It was revived in Victorian times; perhaps influenced by the novel by William Thackerey, *The History of Henry Esmond*, published in 1852.

ETHAN

Means 'firmness' or 'constancy'. A Biblical name which is sometimes found in the United States. Ethan Allen was a prominent figure in the American War of Independence and the name has also been used in fiction.

EUGENE (Owen)

Derives from the Greek meaning 'born lucky'. A popular name in the 19th century inspired by Napoleon's wife – the female form is Eugenie. Mostly given to boys now, it is sometimes shortened to **Gene**.

EUSTACE (Eustis)

Means 'bountiful' or 'fruitful'. A name boosted by the medieval legend of St Eustace, who was converted to Christianity when he saw a vision of the cross.

EVAN

The Welsh form of **John** meaning 'God is gracious'. It has been used since about 1500.

EVERARD (Everett)
Comes from an old German word meaning 'boar'. The
Normans brought the name to England.

EVERETT see **EVERARD**
Believed to be one of the surnames developed from
Everard. It has in recent years been readopted as a
Christian name in this form.

EWAN (Ewen)
Probably derived from the Gaelic for 'youth'. It was
once a common name in England but is now mainly
used by Scottish parents.

EZEKIEL (Zeke)
Means 'God strengthens' in Hebrew. This old Biblical
name was among those often chosen by the Puritans
in the 17th century. It is still found occasionally today,
more especially in the United States where the short
form, **Zeke**, is popular.

EZRA
Means 'help' in Hebrew. Another fine old Biblical
name approved by the 17th-century Puritans. The name
survives today, though rarely, the best-known modern
example being the poet Ezra Pound.

F

FABIEN
From the Latin, meaning 'bean'. The name of an ancient and illustrious Roman family, who listed among their members a historian and a general whose tactics against Hannibal inspired the naming of the Fabien society.

FALKENER
Means 'falcon'. A name adapted from falconer; someone who trains the highly-valued hunting birds.

FELIX
Stems from the Latin word meaning 'happy'. The name was quite widespread in the Middle Ages, it has been the name of four popes and several saints. Although still in general use, it is now rather uncommon.

FERDINAND
Means 'wild' or 'headstrong'. A royal name found in medieval Europe, it was carried to Britain by the Normans and taken up mainly in the Midlands.

FERGUS (Fergie)
Means 'best choice'. It is a form of the Celtic name Feargus, one of the legendary Irish founders of Scotland, and still found mainly in these two countries.

FINN (Finnbarr, Finbar)
Means 'fair' or 'white'. It is an Irish name, a short form of **Finnbarr** or **Finbar**. The legendary Irish hero who defended Ireland with his supernatural powers made this a popular name in Ireland.

FLOYD

Probably developed from the Celtic surname **Lloyd** meaning 'grey' or 'dark' when the English tried to pronounce the difficult 'll' sound. In Britain it is popular with families of West Indian origin.

FORBES

Means 'grazing grass' or 'field'. A Scottish place name adopted as a first name, and chosen mainly in Scotland.

FRANCIS (Frank, Frankie, Franklin)

Derived from the Latin word *Franciscus*, 'Frenchman'. A name kept popular by saints and royals, notably St Francis of Assisi, the patron saint of ecology. It was particularly popular in Britain under the Tudors, then out of favour until the early 19th century.

FRANK

The shortened form of **Francis**. It is, however, a name well recognised in its own right.

FRANKIE

A familiar form of **Francis** and one that has occasionally been recorded as an independent name.

FRANKLIN

Comes from the Norman French for 'freeholder'.

FRASER (Frazer)

Has an uncertain origin but may come from the Old English for 'curly-haired'. It is an old-established Highland surname, only used as a first name over the past 50 years or so, mainly by Scottish parents.

FRED see **ALFRED, FREDERICK**
The shortened form of **Alfred** and of **Frederick,** so
widespread that it must be regarded as a name in its
own right.

FREDERICK (Fredric, Fredrick, Fred, Freddie)
Comes from two Old German words meaning 'peaceful
ruler'. It was one of the most popular boys' names in
the 19th century. Though it is no longer so fashionable,
it remains in frequent currency as a family name, and
it is still quite common in its abbreviated form, **Fred**.

G

GABRIEL (Gabryel, Gabe)
Derives from the Hebrew for 'man of God' and, in the
Bible, it was the name of the Archangel who told the
Virgin Mary that she was to give birth to Christ.

GARETH (Garth, Garret, Gary)
Means 'gentle'. There are varying opinions about the
source of this Welsh name. It is possibly a variant of
Gerard, or from *gwaredd*, 'gentle'. It was first recorded
in England in the 16th century. It is now quite a
common name in Wales.

GARFIELD
Means 'field of spears', stemming from Anglo-Saxon
and was used first as a surname. It was popularised by
the cricketer Sir Garfield Sobers and is widely favoured
by families of West Indian origin.

GARTH see **GARETH**

GARY
Originally an abbreviation of the name Garret, the
ancient version of Gerard meaning 'spear-brave'. It was
popular in the United States around 1950 and became
fashionable in Britain about ten years later.

GAVIN (Gavan, Gaven, Gavyn)
Traces its history to Gawain, from the Welsh meaning
'little hawk' and was the name of one of King Arthur's
distinguished knights. Gavin is the Scottish version.

43

GENE see **EUGENE**

GEOFFREY (Geoff, Jeff, Godfrey, Jefferson, Jeffrey)
Has its origins in Old German and the second half of the name means 'peace'; the first half could come from the words meaning 'god' or 'district'. It was common in the Middle Ages and came back into vogue in the 19th and 20th centuries. The older spelling was **Jeffrey** but Geoffrey is now the more popular form.

GEORGE (Georgie)
Comes from the Greek word for 'farmer'. Though St George is the patron saint of England, it was the four Hanoverian King Georges who popularised the name and it remained a favourite for two centuries. It has been out of fashion in Britain in recent years.

GERAINT
Means 'old'. This medieval Welsh name derives from Gerontius. The Victorian revival of the Arthurian legend of *Geraint* and *Enid* promoted the name.

GERALD (Gerrold, Jerald, Jerold, Gerry, Jerry, Jerrard)
Made up of two Old German words meaning, 'spear' and 'rule'. It is an old-established name but went out of use in England for a period of time. Irish parents continued using the name and it came back into favour in the 19th century.

GERARD (Jerrard, Gerry, Jerry)
Holds similar origins to those of **Gerald** (see above),
two old German words meaning 'spear' and 'brave'.
It was so common in the Middle Ages that it produced
surnames such as Gerrard and Garrett.

GERWYN (Gerwen)
From the Welsh, meaning 'fair'.

GIDEON
Comes from the Hebrew meaning 'one-handed'. It
was one of the Biblical names adopted by the Puritans
in the 17th century and has been used, though not
frequently, ever since.

GILBERT (Gil, Gib, Bert)
Derives from two Old German words meaning
'bright pledge'. It is an old-established name which,
in medieval times, gave rise to surnames such as
Gilbertson, Gilson and Gibbs. It has always been
well liked in Scotland and the north of England.

GILES (Gyles)
It originates from the Greek *Aegidius* meaning 'young
goat' and was made famous by the 7th-century patron
saint of beggars and cripples. There are more than
150 churches in Britain dedicated to him.

GLEN (Glenn)
Began as a surname meaning 'from the valley' in Welsh
and has appeared as a given name for nearly 200 years.
In the 20th century it has often been used as Glenn,
helped by the fame of band-leader Glenn Miller.

GLYN
Comes from the Welsh for 'valley'. Originally exclusive to Wales, this popular Welsh name has now entered general use in England.

GODFREY
Comes from two Old German words and means 'God's peace'. It came to Britain with the Normans and was common in medieval times. In the past it was often confused with Geoffrey but the two names are now quite distinct. Godfrey is rarely used now.

GORDON
Means 'wooded dell'. A Berwickshire place name from which the Scottish clan took its name. The hero General Gordon of Khartoum brought it into use as a Christian name at the end of the 19th century. Since then it has shed its purely Scottish associations and is in general use in all English-speaking countries.

GRAHAM (Grahame, Graeme)
A name which is believed to have originated from the Lincolnshire place name Grantham, and became the surname of a well-known Scottish family. Its use as a Christian name was rare before the 20th century and, until recently, was confined chiefly to those with a Scottish background. This changed after the 1930s when the name was brought into general use in England and became universally popular.

GRANGER
Means 'grainstore'. Once a name for a farm labourer, it was adopted as a first name recently and was popularised by the actor Stewart Granger.

GRANT
Comes from the Old French word meaning, 'great'. Originally a surname only, but like many Scottish surnames adopted in recent years into use first as a middle name (often the mother's maiden name) and later as a full Christian name.

GRAY (Grey, Greyson)
Means 'grey'. The colour may have once referred to grey hair or to the cloaks of the Franciscan and Cistercian monks, known as the Greyfriars.

GREGORY (Greg, Gregg)
A derivative of the Greek word meaning 'to be watchful'. There were two Eastern saints of that name and sixteen popes, including Gregory the Great who sent St Augustine out to convert the English to Christianity. The name has enjoyed a wave of success in the United States and Australia since 1950, but is only now following this trend in Britain.

GRENVILLE
An aristocratic surname, now used as a first name.

GUY
Has uncertain origins, perhaps coming from the Old German meaning 'wood' or 'wide', and was common before the exploits of Guy Fawkes put it out of favour. Though still in general use, Guy has never been a widely popular name in the 20th century.

H

HADDON
Means 'heathland'. An unusual Scottish name, sometimes found as Hadley.

HAL
A diminutive of **Henry**.

HAMILTON
A place name and aristocratic surname, used as a first
name for nearly two hundred years. It is the surname
of the dukes of Abercorn and five other peers.

HAMISH
A pseudo-Gaelic form of **James**, it is a 19th-century
variant frowned on by some purists as an attempt to
emulate the Gaelic **Seamus**. It has come to be used
and pronounced as spelt and it remains a popular
version in Scotland.

HAMMOND
Derived from the German for 'home' and is properly
a surname, used occasionally as a first name, as in the
case of the writer Hammond Innes.

HAMO
Derived from the Old German *haimi*, meaning 'house'
or 'home'. The name came to England with the
Normans and was widely popular at one time, later
evolving into several surnames.

HANK
An American form of **Henry** which is very popular in the United States but unusual in Britain. It is based on the Dutch Henk.

HANS
Means 'God's mercy'. The German and Dutch short form for Johannes, from **John**.

HARLEY
A place name and surname, meaning 'wood with hares', now used as a first name.

HAROLD (Harald, Harrold, Harry)
Derives from two Old English words and means 'ruler of the army'. It was at the height of its popularity in the 19th century. Since then, its popularity has been gradually declining.

HARRISON
A surname, used as a first name since Victorian times.

HARRY
A pet form of **Henry** and an anglicisation of **Henri**, but so well-liked that it is considered as an individual name, particularly since the second son of the Prince and Princess of Wales was given this name.

HARTLEY
A place name meaning 'stag wood', and a surname, now used as a first name.

HARVEY (Harve, Herve)

Originally comes from an Old Breton name meaning 'battle-worthy', and was the name of a 5th-century saint. It was common in the Middle Ages, giving rise to surnames such as Harvey, Hervey and Harveson and came back into favour with Victorian parents, though it is still more popular in the United States.

HAYDEN

Means 'pastureland'. A surname turned first name, perhaps for its pleasant associations with the verdant summer countryside.

HAYDN

From the Celtic meaning 'fire'.

HEATH

A surname which has been taken up in Australia as a boys' Christian name. Heath was originally used as a surname but has become more popular as a Christian name in recent years.

HECTOR

Means 'anchor'. In England, it is the name of the Trojan hero who led the fight against the Greeks for 10 years. In Scotland, where it is more popular, it is a form of the Gaelic *Eachdoin*, meaning 'horse lord'.

HEDLEY

Means 'meadow for sheep'. In Old English dialect, a herder was a young male sheep. A place name adopted as a first name during the 19th century.

HENRY (Hal, Harry, Hank, Henri, Hendrick, Heriot)

From the Old German meaning, 'home-ruler'. An old name that has remained in fashion for centuries and was given to eight kings of England. **Harry**, now used as a pet form or an independent name, was the original English version of the name, with Henry taking over in the 17th century.

HERBERT (Bert, Bertie, Herb, Herbie)

Comes from the Old German meaning 'bright army'. It was popular at the end of the 19th century but has been little used in recent times.

HERMAN

This is an Old German name from two words meaning 'army' and 'man'. Still thought of as a German name it is sometimes used in Britain. The name is more common in the United States.

HIRAM

Comes from the Hebrew and means 'exalted brother'. It was first used as a name in the 17th century by the Puritans but it has not been widely used in recent years.

HOMER

The Greek name meaning 'pledge', or Anglo-Saxon, 'pool in a hollow'. This old name with its poetic associations is rarely used in England but it does sometimes appear in the United States.

HORACE and HORATIO

Originated from a renowned Roman family, Horatius. Horatio came into use from the middle of the 16th century. By the 18th century the French form, Horace, was more general.

HOWARD (Howie)
Comes from a surname with an aristocratic pedigree as the family name of the Dukes of Norfolk, but its origins are uncertain; it may mean either 'protection' or 'heart'. It has come into general use as a Christian name in the last 100 years or so, unaffected by changes in fashion.

HOWELL (Hoel, Howel)
Means 'eminent'. This anglicised form of the Welsh name Hywel may also come from the English place name meaning, 'hill for swine'.

HUDSON
A surname meaning 'son of hudd' or 'Hugh', now used as a first name.

HUGH (Hew, Huw, Hugo, Hubert, Hughie)
From the Old German meaning 'mind' it came to England with the Normans in the Latin form **Hugo**. It was made popular by the learned 11th-century bishop St Hugh of Lincoln and stayed in fashion for the next 500 years. Other related forms are the Latin versions **Hugo** and **Hubert**, which mean 'bright mind'; both are in common use throughout Britain.

HUMPHREY
May be derived from the Old German 'giant peace' or be of Anglo-Saxon origin, the first part meaning, 'honey'. Humphrey had almost died out by the 19th century. Then a revival took place and today the name is quite well known.

IAN (Iain, Ion)
A modern version of **John** meaning 'God is gracious'.
It soon spread beyond Scotland to become a favourite
all over Britain.

IDRIS
An old Welsh name meaning 'fiery lord' still commonly
used in Wales.

IFOR see **IVOR**

INIGO
A Spanish version of the name Ignatius, regularly used
in Great Britain.

IRVING and **IRWIN (Irvine, Erwin)**
These names are taken from the Anglo-Saxon 'boar-
friend' and are examples of a surname being used as a
first name. Towards the end of the 19th century Irving
was sometimes used as a Christian name.

ISAAC (Izaak)
Stems from the Hebrew word meaning 'laughter' and
appears in the Old Testament as the name of the son
of Abraham and Sarah. It was at its most popular with
other Biblical names in the 17th century. It is now
regarded as a chiefly Jewish name and is not so widespread as it was at the beginning of the 20th century.

IVAN
The Russian version of **John** meaning 'God is gracious',
which has been adopted by English-speaking parents in

modern times and is now quite well known. The feminine form, Ivanna, is rarely used.

IVO (Ives)
From the German, meaning 'yew wood'. A popular name in Normandy, it was brought to England during the Norman Conquest.

IVOR (Ifor)
An old-established Celtic name although its meaning is uncertain. It gave rise to Scottish surnames such as MacIvor and MacIver. Welsh parents use **Ifor**, which means 'lord'.

JACK

A form of **John,** and not derived from the French
Jacques (**James**) as it is sometimes thought. The name
went through an interesting process of evolution from
Johannes through to Jehan, Jan (the popular form of
John in the Low Countries) and Jankin (with the
Flemish suffix). The French pronunciation of Jankin
sounded like Jackin and led to the shortened form, Jack.
It has remained in constant use in place of John, and as
an independent name, but though still very common it
is no longer the favourite it was in the 1950s.

JACOB (Jackson, Jacques, Jago, Jake, James)

Comes from the Hebrew for 'supplanter'; in the Old
Testament Jacob tricked his brother Esau out of his
inheritance. It came into general use after the
Reformation, through now it is mainly used by Jewish
families. Today the short form **Jake** is used as an
independent name.

JAGO

The Cornish version of **James.**

JAMES (Jim, Jimmy, Hamis, Jaimie, Jamie, Jas, Jay)

Developed from the name **Jacob** (see above), meaning
'supplanter'. Though there were two apostles called
James, it only became popular once James Stuart
became King of England in 1603. **Jamie** is one of the
abbreviated forms of James which is now used as a
name in its own right, both for boys and girls.

JARED (Jarod, Jareth)
Comes from the Hebrew meaning 'rose' and has been used regularly, though not frequently, as given names for boys since the 17th century.

JARROD
An old surname derived from **Gerald**, now used as a first name.

JARVIS
A surname derived from Gervase, now used as a first name.

JASON
Jason is the English form of the Greek name of the writer of the *Book of Ecclesiasticus*. The meaning is uncertain; possibly 'healer' from the Greek. It first became popular in The United States and was a favourite in Britain during the 20th century.

JASPER (Casper, Gasper)
Means 'imperial' or 'precious'. The origin is unknown, through it probably comes from the East. This is the English form of the German name **Casper**.

JAY
Comes from the bird name which in English and Old French meant 'chattering'.

JEDIDIAH (Jed)
A Hebrew name meaning 'friend of Jehovah'. The short form, **Jed**, is more often used today.

JEFFERSON (Jeff)
Comes from the surname meaning 'son of Godffrey' and was first used by American parents after Thomas Jefferson, only spreading to Britain in recent years.

JEREMY (Jeremiah, Jerry, Jerrie)
Has the grand meaning 'God exalts', stemming from the Hebrew and in modern times has taken over in popularity from the more formal **Jeremiah**. Both are shortened to **Jerry**, which is also used as an independent name.

JEROME (Jerry, Jerrie)
Means 'holy name' in Greek. St Jerome (340-420 AD) was the translator of the Latin version of the Bible, accepted as the authorised version of the Roman Catholic Church. Today Jerome is unusual in Britain.

JESSE (Jess)
Comes from the Hebrew meaning 'the Lord exists' and, in the Old Testament is the name of King David's father. It was first used by parents after the Reformation and has survived the generations. It was popularised in the 20th century by the athlete Jesse Owens.

JETHRO (Jeth, Jett)
Means 'abundance'. A biblical name and that of the English inventor and agriculturalist Jethro Tull (1647-1741).

JOACHIM

From the Hebrew, meaning 'may Jehovah exult'. Legend gives this name to the father of the Blessed Virgin Mary. It has been used in England since the 13th century.

JOB

From the Hebrew, meaning 'persecuted'. In the Old Testament he endured great suffering with exemplary patience.

JOE see JOSEPH

The shortened form of **Joseph** used sometimes as an independent name, particularly in the United States and Canada.

JOEL

Comes from the Hebrew 'Jehovah is the Lord' and was the name of one of the minor prophets of the Old Testament. The Normans brought it to Britain as a personal name.

JOHN (Johnny, Jon, Jan, Jake, Jack)

Comes from the Hebrew Jochanaan (Johanan) meaning 'God is gracious'. The Latin form Johannes was brought from the East by the Crusaders and is the name of Christ's cousin, John the Baptist. Throughout the centuries, John has remained one of the most popular Christian names, not only in Britain but in other countries as well.

JOLYON See JULIAN

JONAS (Jonah)
From the Hebrew word for 'dove'. It is the favoured
form of Jonah, the name of the Old Testament prophet
which became associated with bad luck. It has survived
the generations without ever being particularly popular.

JONATHAN (Jonathon, Jonothon, Jon, Jonathoan)
Derives from a Hebrew word that means 'gift of God'.
In the Old Testament it is the name of King David's
close friend. It has been widely used in England since
the Reformation and is quite popular today.

JORDAN
The name of the principal river in Israel, where Christ
was baptised by John the Baptist.

JOSEPH (Jo, Joe, Joey, Josepth)
Means 'may the Lord add' in Hebrew and is the New
Testament name for the husband of the Virgin Mary
and Joseph of Arimathea. At first it was used mainly
by Jewish families but by the 19th century it was widespread and it has been a favourite in Britain and the
United States in recent times.

JOSHUA (Josh, Jesus, Jason)
Comes from the Hebrew meaning 'God saves' and is
another form of the name **Jesus**. It has become popular
in English-speaking countries in the past few years and
is abbreviated to **Josh**.

JOSIAH
From the Hebrew, meaning 'God heals'.

JUDE

Means 'prize'. St Jude is patron saint of lost causes. The name was promoted by Thomas Hardy's novel *Jude the Obscure* (1895).

JULIAN (Jolin, Jolyon, Jules)

Comes originally from the Latin name Julius which meant 'downy' or 'hairy' and is the name of many saints, but it has only been used widely by parents during the 20th century.

JUSTIN

Derives from the Latin for 'righteous' and is an old-established name which was used by Irish parents before it shot into fashion all over the English-speaking world in the past decade.

KANE
An unusual boys' name which comes from the Welsh
'beautiful', or Manx 'warrior'.

KARL see **CHARLES, CARL**

KEGAN
An unusual boys' name which is the Irish equivalent
of **Hugh,** and has been said to mean 'little fiery one'.

KEIR
From the Gaelic, meaning 'swarthy'. A surname now
used as a first name.

KEITH
Comes originally from a Scottish place name which
may mean 'wind' or 'wood'. It was taken up as a family
name and spread to England as a first name at the turn
of the century, becoming widely used.

KELSEY (Kelcey)
An English place name and surname, used as a first
name since the 1870s.

KELVIN (Kelvyn)
Originally the name of a Scottish river, possibly meaning
'narrow stream', used as a given name since the middle
of the 1950s.

KENDALL
A place name, meaning 'valley of the River Kent', and a
surname. Used as a first name in mid-Victorian times.

KENNETH (Ken, Kenny)

Comes from an old Gaelic word meaning 'handsome'. It was popular with Scottish parents from the time of Kenneth MacAlpine, the first king of Scotland. Over the past 100 years it has been used widely, making its biggest impact in Britain in the 1920s, and has lost its strong Scottish associations.

KENT

Means 'chief', or possibly 'white' or 'bright' in Celtic. It is also a place name. This surname is now an accepted Christian name in Canada and the United States, where it has become quite popular.

KESTER

An abbreviation of **Christopher** popular in the 17th century and now enjoying a revival.

KEVIN (Coemgen, Kevan, Kevyn)

This is a Gaelic name meaning 'comely at birth' and made popular by St Kevin, the 10th-century abbot of Glendalough in County Wicklow. It was common among Irish families long before it spread more widely in the 1900s and became a favourite with British and American parents.

KIERAN (Kieron, Kieren)

Means 'black' in Irish, that is, dark-skinned or dark-haired. It occurs in Ireland but is little used elsewhere.

KINGSLEY

Means 'King's wood' or 'meadow'. A surname turned first name in the late 19th century, promoted today by the novelist Kingsley Amis.

KIRK
Taken from the surname meaning 'church', it has been used as a Christian name for over 100 years.

KURT (Curt)
This is the diminutive of the German name Konrad, meaning 'bold counsel', used in Britain in recent years as a name in its own right.

KYLE
A Gaelic name used for both boys and girls, meaning 'handsome'.

L

LACHLAN
From the Gaelic meaning 'warlike'.

LAMBERT
Means 'bright as the land'. A popular name in the Middle Ages, honouring the Flemish saint; it has seen a revival in recent years.

LANCE
Derived from the Old German word meaning 'land' and is the short form of Lancelot, a name made famous through the hero from the Arthurian legends. Lancelot was used by 19th-century parents but has now almost disappeared.

LAURENCE (Lawrence, Laruence, Laurie, Lars, Larry, Larkin)
The Latin name Laurentus is probably derived from *laurus*, 'bay tree'. The 3rd-century martyr St Laurence, Archdeacon of Rome, later gave his name to the St Laurence River in Canada.

LEE
Originally a surname from the Anglo-Saxon for 'meadow'. It was first used as a personal name by American parents, and has become popular in Britain. It is usually a boys' name but can also be used for girls.

LEIGHTON
From the Old English, meaning 'herb garden'. A place name and surname, used as a first name since the 1800s.

LEO
Comes from the Latin for 'lion'. Thirteen popes have taken the name so it has always been favoured by Roman Catholic parents, while Jewish families prefer the form Leon.

LEONARD (Len, Lenny, Lennie)
Derived from the Old German name Leonhard, meaning 'lion' and 'brave'. It was not very common until the first quarter of the 20th century, when it rose sharply in popularity. Now, although still in widespread use, it is no longer so fashionable.

LEOPOLD
From the German, meaning 'people behold'. The name became popular in Britain in the 19th century.

LEROY
Comes from the Old French meaning 'the king'. Until recent times it was regarded as an American name but it is now frequently used in Britain by families of West Indian origin.

LESLIE
Originally a Scottish place name, probably meaning 'little meadow', it has been taken up as a surname. In use as a first name for both boys and girls since the 18th century and though the usual masculine form is **Leslie** and the feminine **Lesley**, the spellings are interchangeable.

LESTER
A surname taken from the place name, Leicester. It is sometimes used as a first name, especially in the United States and Australia.

LEWIS (Lew)

The anglicised version of the name **Louis** meaning 'famous in war'. Welsh parents have used the name regularly as an alternative for Llewellyn and it was brought to public attention in England by Lewis Carroll, author of *Alice in Wonderland*.

LIAM

An Irish version of **William** meaning 'helmet', which has been taken up by non-Irish parents.

LINDSAY

It is derived from a place name 'Lindon's Isle' in Lincolnshire and was first used as a given name by Scottish parents, first for boys, then for both boys and girls.

LIONEL

Is a French diminutive form of Leon, meaning 'young lion'. Edward III's son bore the name and it has occurred periodically since, especially in the North of England.

LLEWELLYN (Llywelyn, Llew, Lyn)

A Celtic name which means 'like a lion' and is a long established favourite in Wales, though its use has declined in recent years.

LLOYD

Traces its descent from the Welsh word for 'grey' and is a common surname and popular as a first name, having spread to families without Welsh connections early in the 20th century.

LOGAN
From the Gaelic, meaning 'small hollow'. A Scottish place name and surname, now used as a first name.

LOUIS (Lewis, Lou)
Means 'glorious in war'. Louis is the French form of **Lewis** and the one which has become more firmly established in the United States. It is now also increasingly preferred in England, including the French pronunciation.

LUCAS, LUKE
Comes from the Greek, Loukas, 'man of Luciana', the name of St Luke the Evangelist. Lucas is the Latinised form which reached England about the 12th century. Neither Lucas nor Luke has ever been an outstanding favourite in Britain, but there are signs that both are rising in popularity.

LUCIEN
Means 'shining out'. Derived from Lucius.

LUDOVIC
The Latin version of **Louis**.

LUTHER
Comes from the Old German word for 'famous army' and is associated with the 16th-century religious reformer Martin Luther.

LYLE
An unusual boy's name derived from old French meaning 'island'.

LYNDON
From the Old English, meaning 'lime-tree hill'. A place name and surname, now used as a first name.

LYNTON (Linton)
From the Old English, meaning 'place on the torrent'. A place name and surname, now used as a first name.

MAGNUS (Manus)
Comes from the Latin meaning 'great' or 'noble', and
it has been widely used in Scandinavia, the Shetland
Islands, Scotland and Ireland.

MALCOLM
Comes from the Gaelic meaning 'servant of St Columba'.
It has been a favourite in Scotland, with four Scottish
kings bearing the name, and in modern times has been
in widespread use.

MARK (Marc, Marcel, March, Marcus, Marion, Marius)
Derives from the name of the Roman god of war, Mars,
and means 'war-like'. It was the name of the author of
one of the Gospels but it is only in the past 30 years
that it has become one of the most popular boys' names
in the English-speaking world.

MARLEY
From the Old English, meaning 'pleasant wood'. A
place name and surname, now used as a first name.

MARSHALL
Comes from the French-German word for 'farrier', and
is a surname which has become popular as a first name
in the United States.

MARTIN (Marty, Martyn)
Comes, like **Mark** (see above) from Mars, the god of
war. It was a common name in the Middle Ages, giving
rise to surnames such as Martin, Martinson and Martel

and has survived through the centuries to be a popular choice until quite recently.

MASON
An old occupational surname, now used as a first name.

MATTHEW (Matthias, Mat, Matty, Mathias, Matias, Matt, Mattie)
Comes from Hebrew meaning 'gift of God' and was so common in the Middle Ages that it produced surnames such as Macey, Matthews and Mayhew. It came back into fashion with the present generation to become one of the most popular boys' names.

MAURICE (Morris)
Comes from the Latin *mauritius* 'a moor'. It was most frequently used by British parents in the first half of the 20th century, often as Morris.

MAXIMILIAN (Maxim, Maxwel)
Comes from the Latin title of honour meaning 'greatest' and was a favourite name in Germany before spreading to Britain.

MAXWELL (Max, Maxie, Maxy)
Comes from Anglo-Saxon and Scottish place names, meaning 'large spring'. This surname has come into widespread use as a personal name in the 20th century.

MAYNARD
Means 'very strong'.

MELVIN (Melvyn, Mel)
Possibly from the Gaelic *Malvin*, 'smooth brow', or a

place name. It is also suggested it could be from the Celtic *Melva*, meaning 'chief'.

MERLIN
Means 'sea hill' in Old Welsh and was the name of King Arthur's magician. The name is uncommon today.

MERVYN (Mervin, Marvin, Merv)
From the same Old Welsh word as **Merlin** meaning 'sea hill'.

MICHAEL (Mick, Mickey, Mike)
Derives from the Hebrew meaning 'who is like god'. It has always been a favourite name, and is so common in Ireland that 'Mick' has become a nickname for any Irishman. It has been one of the most fashionable names this century.

MILES (Myle, Milo)
Has uncertain origins but may mean 'beloved'. It is an old-established name brought to England by the Normans and has been used fairly steadily through the years.

MILTON
An Anglo-Saxon name for 'mill enclosure' and a surname used occasionally as a first name.

MITCHELL (Mitch)
A surname derived from the medieval French version of **Michael**, now used as a first name.

MONTAGUE (Monty, Monte)
Originally from a French place name meaning 'pointed

71

hill', it came to Britain as a surname with the Norman invasion.

MORGAN
From the Welsh, meaning 'sea-bright'. A surname, now used as a first name for boys and girls.

MORTIMER
A French place name and surname, now used as a first name.

MORTON
An Old English place name, meaning 'farm on the fen', used as a first name since the 19th century.

MOSES (Moshe, Moss, Moy)
Means 'saved' and 'saviour'. Hidden among bulrushes as a baby to save his life, this biblical hero led the Israelites out of Egypt and received the Ten Commandments from God. A name always popular with Jewish families.

MUNGO
This is the Celtic nickname meaning 'most dear' for St Kentigern, founder of the church in Glasgow.

MUNRO
A Scottish surname, now used as a first name.

MURDOCH (Murdo)
From the Gaelic, meaning 'sailor'. A surname now used as a first name.

MURPHY
Means 'of the sea'. This Celtic name is an Irish
favourite, even though Murphy's Law states that if
anything can go wrong, it will.

MURRAY (Moray)
A Celtic clan name, possibly taken from the Moray
Firth, which is sometimes taken as a personal name.

MYRON
A boys' name dating back to the days of ancient Greece
and means 'fragrant'.

N

NAPOLEON
Means 'new town'.

NATHAN (Nat, Natty)
Means 'gift' in Hebrew. In the Old Testament Nathan was a prophet. The name was occasionally used by the Puritans in the 17th century and subsequently occurred from time to time. However apart from a brief period in fashion in the United States around 1900, it has received little attention.

NATHANIEL (Nat, Nath)
Means 'God has given' in Hebrew and was one of the Biblical names that came into use after the Reformation, though it has never been a favourite.

NED
A pet form of **Edward**. Common in the Middle Ages, it is now enjoying a revival.

NEIL (Neill, Neal, Niall, Niull, Nelly)
Probably comes from the Old Irish for 'champion' and was popular in Scotland long before it was taken up all over Britain, where it has been in fashion for the past 30 years.

NELSON
Began as a surname meaning 'Nell's son' and came into fashion as a personal name in honour of the hero of Trafalgar, Lord Nelson.

NEVILLE

A Norman surname taken from a place name, Neuville, in France. The Nevilles were a powerful family in the Middle Ages and the name first appears as a Christian name as early as the 17th century. It was not until the 20th century that it became fully acceptable as a personal name and it is now quite widespread.

NICHOLAS (Nicolas, Nicky, Nick, Nico, Klaus, Nic)

Derives from the Greek name Nicolaus meaning 'victory' and 'people'. Common in the Middle Ages it has survived the centuries to become popular in many English-speaking countries in recent years.

NIGEL

From the same root as **Neil** meaning 'champion', it has been popular with British parents in recent times.

NINIAN

An unusual boys' name. The source of this name is uncertain. It may possibly be of Celtic origin, or perhaps a corruption of **Vivian**, from the Latin *vivus*, 'alive', though this seems unlikely.

NOAH

Derives from the Hebrew for 'long lived' or possibly 'repose', and as one of the oldest Biblical names has been in use for centuries, though it is uncommon today.

NOEL (Noelle)

From the French for Christmas', and from Latin *natalis* (*dies*), or 'birth(day)'. Since the 13th century Noel has been given as a Christian name to children of both sexes who were born at Christmas time.

75

NOLAN

An Irish surname, meaning 'descendant of a noble', now used as a first name.

NORBERT

From the Old German, meaning 'famous in the north'.

NORMAN (Norm)

Comes from the Old English name for a 'man from the north' and appears in the Domesday Book. It survived the generations in Scotland and became established once more in the rest of Britain during the 20th century.

NORRIS

From the Old French meaning 'northerner'. First used as a surname, now in use as a first name.

OLIVER (Olly)
Has uncertain origins but may stem from a Teutonic name meaning 'elf-host'. It is an old-established name which went out of favour with Oliver Cromwell, only returning to regular use during the 20th century.

OMAR
Means 'long life' or 'most high'. Introduced to Britain when the medieval Persian poet Omar Khayyam's *Ruba'iyat* was published in English in 1859.

ORLANDO see **ROLAND**

ORSON
Comes from the Latin word for 'bear'. The English equivalent of the Italian Orso, it is well known because of the fame of Orson Wells, actor and film-maker.

ORVILLE
Comes from a French place name meaning 'gold town'. It is best known as the name of the pioneer aviator Orville Wright.

OSBERT
Means 'shining god'. A name originally confined to the north of England where Os had been the prefix of the Northumbrian rulers, but revived throughout Britain during the 19th century.

OSCAR (Os, Ossy, Ossie)
Comes from the old English words for 'god' and 'spear'. After Napoleon's godson of that name became king of Sweden the name spread through Europe. Oscar Wilde

is still probably the most famous bearer of the name.

OSMOND
Means 'God's protection'. A name made popular by St Osmund, who was William the Conqueror's Chancellor and Bishop of Salisbury, to be revived with other old names in the 19th century.

OSWALD
Means 'God of the woods' or 'God of power'.

OTIS
Means 'keen eared' in Greek; or possibly from Old German *Otho* 'wealthy'. Not a well-known name in Britain, it occasionally occurs in the United States, where in recent years it has been used as a girls' name as well as a boys'.

OTTO
Means 'prosperous'. A German royal name that has never been popular in Britain.

OWEN (Owain)
Believed to be from the Latin *Eugenius*, 'well-born', though it is sometimes thought to have been derived from the Welsh word *oen*, 'lamb'. The name has been in common use for so long that it has lost most of its exclusively Welsh associations and is to be found everywhere in the English-speaking world.

PASCAL (Pascale, Pascow, Pascoe, Pask)
It is derived from the French name for Easter.

PARIS
The name of the romantic Greek hero whose elopement with Helen caused the Trojan war.

PATRICK (Pat, Paddy, Padraig, Paris, Patrice, Pattison, Paxton, Peter, Peyton)
Comes from the Latin word *patricius* meaning 'nobleman' and was made famous by the 5th-century patron saint of Ireland. It has always been so popular there that 'Paddy' has become a nickname for an Irishman but the name is also widely used in Britain and the United States.

PAUL
Derives from Latin and means 'small'. In spite of being the name adopted by St Paul in the New Testament, it failed to catch the imagination of parents. It has become one of the top fashionionable names of the past 20 years.

PERCIVAL
Means 'warrior of fire'. A medieval French name, given to one of King Arthur's legendary knights, and revived by the Victorian medievalists. Less common today.

PERCY
Comes from the name of a place in Normandy. The Northumbrian family of that name were associates of William the Conqueror. The name was generally used until the end of the 19th century but seems now to have faded out.

PEREGRINE

Means 'traveller' or 'pilgrim'. An early Christian name popular under the Hanoverians.

PERRY

Began as the short form of **Peregrine**, from the Latin for 'a traveller' but has been a name in its own right for over a century.

PETER (Pete)

Stems from the Greek word meaning 'a rock'. It was the name given to Jesus' disciple Simon. Out of favour after the Reformation the name came back into fashion in the 20th century.

PHILIP (Pip, Phip, Phil)

Is from the Greek meaning 'fond of horses'. The name of one of Christ's disciples acquired royal character through Spanish and French kings but, like Peter, was ousted by the Protestants.

PIERS (Pearce, Pierce, Peers, Pierre)

Is an early French version of **Peter**, meaning 'rock', which came to England with the Normans. It is still used frequently by parents.

PRESTON

An Old English place name, meaning 'priest's farm', and surname, used as a first name since the 19th century. It is the surname of the viscounts Gormanston.

PRICE

A surname meaning 'son of Rhys', now generally used as a first name.

PRINCE

Means 'chief'. This Roman name was adopted as a British surname given to black American slaves. Only used as a first name during the 20th century, but still not widely used today.

Q

QUENTIN (Quintin)
Originates from the Latin *quinctus*, meaning 'fifth', and from the name of a Roman clan. It came to Britain at the time of the Norman Conquest and was used periodically up to the 13th century and much later in Scotland, where it was equated with a Celtic name. Though it still survives it has never been widespread.

R

RALEIGH
Means 'deer's pasture'. A name honouring Sir Walter Raleigh, a favourite of Queen Elizabeth I.

RALPH (Rafe, Ralf, Ralston, Randolph, Raoul)
Comes from the Anglo-Saxon word meaning 'Courageous adviser' and is a name which has survived from ancient times, pronounced Rafe until quite recently. It made its biggest impact early this century.

RALSTON
A place name and surname, used as a first name since the 19th century.

RAMSAY
Means 'sheep's or raven's island'. This ancient Scottish surname became a first name and was made better known by James Ramsay MacDonald (1866-1937), Britain's first Labour Prime Minister.

RANDAL (Randall, Ranulf, Randy)
A very old name derived from two Anglo-Saxon words meaning 'shield' and 'wolf'. In the Middle Ages it gave rise to surnames like Randal, Randle and Rason. By the 18th century **Randolph** had appeared as a variation.

RANDOLPH
Means 'courageous protector'. Popular as **Randal** in the Middle Ages, this name was given to the statesman Randolph Churchill (1849-95), Winston Churchill's father.

RAOUL

The French form of the old version of **Ralph**. It is occasionally used in English-speaking countries.

RAYMOND (Raymund, Ray)

Derives from two Old German words meaning 'counsel' and 'protection' and came to England with the Normans. Parents used it sparingly during the 20th century when it came into vogue in most English-speaking countries.

REGINALD (Reg, Rex)

From two Old English words meaning 'power' and 'force' and in early times the name appeared as **Reynold**. Its use faded out, but was revived in the 19th century.

REID (Reed)

Comes from the Old English word for red. It is a surname which has come into use as a first name, particularly in the United States.

REUBEN (Rube, Ruben)

Means 'behold a son' in Hebrew. A son of Jacob bore this name and it was one of the Biblical names adopted by the Puritans in the 17th century. In Britain it has come to be regarded as a mainly Jewish name.

REX

Means 'king' in Latin. This was originally an abbreviated form of **Reginald**, but in modern usage it is regarded as a separate name and has almost lost its earlier associations.

REYNOLD see REGINALD

RHYS (Reece)
Means 'rash' or 'impetuous' and has always been a
favourite Welsh name which has produced surnames
like Rees and Rice.

**RICHARD (Dick, Dicky or Dickie, Rick, Ricky,
Richie, Hick, Hudd, Hudson, Rocco)**
Believed to be from the Old German name Ricohard,
though there had been an Anglo-Saxon name Ricehard,
meaning 'rule hard'. It is so deeply entrenched as one
of the most commonplace in English life that it has
been little affected through the centuries by fashionable
trends. **Dick**, the favourite abbreviation, was used, like
Jack, to stand for Everyman.

**ROBERT (Bob, Bobby, Bobbie, Rob, Robin,
Robbie)**
Comes from the Old German Hrodebert, from *hrothi*,
'fame', and *berhta*, 'bright'. There was an Anglo-Saxon
name, Hreodbeorht, already in existence when the
Normans brought Robert, the French derivation from
Germany, to England. After the Norman Conquest the
name became extremely popular, appearing in many
forms and shortened versions. To the present day it has
remained one of the most firmly established of all our
names, a universal favourite, untouched by the fluctua-
tions of fashion.

ROBIN (Robyn)
Although this was originally a diminutive of **Rob**, the
abbreviated form of **Robert**, it has been accepted since
the 13th century as an independent name. Since the
middle of the 20th century Robin has enjoyed a certain
renewal of favour after a period in eclipse.

RODERICK (Rod, Roddy, Roddie)

Derives from the Old German Hrodric, from *hrothi*, 'fame', and *ricja*, 'rule'. In Scotland it became confused with the Gaelic name Rharidh, 'red', which was then rendered by Roderick, and the name is still traditional in certain clans. In the present century it is no longer confined to Scotland but is a well-known name in most English-speaking countries.

RODNEY (Rod, Roddie, Roddy)

This was originally a surname taken from a place name meaning 'reed island'. It is quite common, though usually found nowadays in an abbreviated form.

ROGER

Comes from the Anglo-Saxon Hrothgar, from *hrothi*, 'fame', and *ger*, 'spear'. The Anglo-Saxon name became merged with the French, Roger, brought over by the Normans. By the 18th century, the name had come to be associated chiefly with rustic simplicity, though it remained traditional in some families. It returned to favour at the end of the 19th century and is still in widespread use.

ROHAN

A French place name and aristocratic surname, now used as a first name.

ROLAND (Rowland, Rolland)

Comes from the Old German Hrodland, from *hrothi*, 'fame', and *landa*, 'land'. This was the name of Charlemagne's champion, the subject of the French epic poem, *La Chanson de Roland*. There is an old Scottish ballad entitled *Childe Rowland* about King

Arthur's son, whose sister is carried away by the fairies.
Roland has always been a name with romantic
associations.

ROLF (Rollo, Rudolf)
Means 'famous for bravery'. The Normans introduced
this form of the German name Hrodult, but it was
revived in its full form, Rudolph, last century.

RONALD (Ranald, Ron, Ronnie)
Stems from an Old Norse name R^gnvaldrand meaning
'power' and 'force'. This is the Scottish equivalent of
Reynold, the old form of **Reginald**, but it has been
common outside Scotland for so long that it is no
longer thought of as a Scottish name.

RONAN
From the Irish, meaning 'little seal'. The Irish St Ronan
worked as a missionary in Cornwall in the 5th century.
He was later consecrated Bishop by St Patrick.

RORY (Rauri)
The anglicised form of the Gaelic Ruairidh, meaning
'red'. It was confined to Scotland and Ireland until this
century.

ROSS
This is probably a place name from the Celtic meaning
'promontory'. Other origins suggested have been from
the Germanic 'fame', French 'red', or from the Anglo-
Saxon 'horse'. Originally a Scottish surname, it was
brought into general use as a Christian name only in
the 20th century. It is fairly widespread in Scotland,
Australia and Canada.

ROWAN
Rowan is becoming increasingly popular as a name for girls or boys. It comes from the Rowan tree, which was believed to have the power to drive away evil.

ROY
Comes from the Gaelic *ruahd*, meaning 'red', though it is often believed to come from the French *roi*, meaning 'king'. Originally a Scottish name, it is by no means confined to Scotland, and since the beginning of the present century has been distributed generally throughout the English-speaking world.

ROYSTON
A surname taken from the Yorkshire place name. It has been recorded as a personal name in the 18th century and occasionally in our own time, but it is fairly rare and confined chiefly to England and Australia.

RUFUS
Comes from the Latin for red-haired and was originally used by Jewish families as an alternative to **Reuben**. It is now in common use particularly in the United States.

RUPERT
Comes from the Old German Hrodebert, meaning 'fame bright', the same root as for **Robert**. It first became familiar in England during the Civil War when the Royal cause was gallantly defended by Prince Rupert of the Rhine. In the present century it has again been associated with gallantry through the poet Rupert Brooke, who died tragically during the First World War. With such a distinguished record it is almost surprising to find the name in use today.

RUSSELL (Russel, Russ, Rusty)
Comes from a surname which, in turn, derives from the French, *roux*, for 'red'. It has been fairly popular with British parents in recent years.

RYAN
Means 'little king'. It is a modern first name taken from an Irish surname. It has in recent years been adopted as a Christian name and become immensely popular.

S

SAMSON
Means 'sun'. The name of the biblical judge and strong-man was given to a popular Welsh saint. Revived after the Reformation, but not widely in use now.

SAMUEL (Sam, Sammie, Sammy)
Means 'heard by God', or 'name of God'. It occurred occasionally from the 12th century onwards, and appeared as a surname. But it was after the Reformation, when the Bible became a rich source of Christian names, that it really came into general use.

SANDY
The medieval pet form of **Alexander**, now considered an independent name. It was particularly popular in Scotland.

SAUL
Means 'asked for' in Hebrew and appears in the Bible as the first king of Israel and Saul of Tarsus, who became St Paul.

SCOTT
Comes from a surname meaning 'a Scotsman' and has only been used as a personal name during the 20th century, becoming very successful in both Scotland, England and the United States over the past 20 years.

SEAMUS (Seumas, Seumus, Shamus)
Means 'supplanter'. This Irish form of **James** gained favour in mainland Britain in the 1950s.

SEAN (Shaun, Shawn)

Is the Irish form of **John,** meaning 'God is gracious'. It evolved through the Old French name Jehan, modern French Jean, and is equivalent to the Irish Gaelic name Eoin, which is itself returning to use in Ireland. More than other Irish male names, Sean is quite often found outside Ireland, though it is usually confined to families with Irish connections.

SEBASTIAN (Seb, Sebastien, Steb)

Derives from Greek meaning 'majestic' or the Latin meaning 'man of sebatia' and was made famous by the martyred 3rd-century saint. It was a popular medieval name which later fell out of favour and was only revived during the 20th century.

SELWYN

Comes from the Anglo-Saxon for 'close-friend' and began as a surname. An English name, but mostly found in Wales where it takes on the Welsh meaning, 'fair zeal'.

SERGE

Means 'servant'. A French form of a Roman family name, used as Sergei for the two Russian composers Rachmaninoff and Prokofiev.

SETH

Means 'appointed'. The name of Adam and Eve's third son became popular under the Hanoverians and gained some favour in the 19th century with George Eliot's novel *Adam Bede* (1859).

SEYMOUR
A French place name and aristocratic surname, now used as a first name. It is the surname of the dukes of Somerset.

SHANE see SEAN

SHELDON
An Anglo-Saxon name meaning 'from the hill ledge'. It is a surname that has begun to be used as a first name.

SHERIDAN
Evolved as a surname which was used as a boys' first name for 100 years, with parents showing more interest since writer Sheridan Morley publicised it.

SHERLOCK (Sherman, Sherwood, Woody)
Means 'area of land'. A name made popular in the last century by Sir Arthur Conan Doyle's fictional detective, Sherlock Holmes.

SHOLTO
From the Gaelic, meaning 'sower'.

SIDNEY (Sydney, Sid, Syd)
Means 'God of the Nysa'. Believed to be a contraction of the French 'St Denis', it is the surname of a famous English family. By the end of the 19th century it had become very common and though it is still widely used it is no longer so popular.

SILAS
From the Aramaic, meaning 'asked of God'. In the New Testament, Silas, a Roman citizen, accompanied Paul

on his second journey to Corinth. The name came into use after the Reformation.

SILVESTER
Means 'wood'. Three popes ensured the popularity of this name in medieval Europe.

SIMON (Silas, Sim, Simeon, Simpson, Sims)
Comes from the Hebrew Shimeon, 'hearkening'. This is the Greek form of the name, which literally means 'snub nose'. It occurs in the New Testament and was popular in England in the Middle Ages as the name of the Apostle, Simon Peter. Both **Simeon** and Simon were the name of several saints. As a saint's name it lost favour after the Reformation and was relegated to the poorer sections of society, a reminder of which may be seen in the nursery rhyme 'Simple Simon'. In the 20th century it recovered and rose in popularity in the 1970s.

SINCLAIR
Means 'shining brightly'. An anglicised form of the French name St Clair, and in use since the 19th century when given to the writer Sinclair Lewis (1885-1951).

SOLOMON (Sol, Solly)
Means 'little man of peace', or 'worshipper of Shalman' in Hebrew. It is regarded as a chiefly Jewish name.

SPENCER
Originally a surname meaning 'dispenser'. It belonged to a very distinguished family and was first adopted as a personal name by their descendants and associates. In the 20th century it became more common, and in recentl years has appeared more frequently.

SPIKE
Means 'point' or 'ear of corn'.

STANFORD (Stamford)
An English place name, meaning 'stony meadow', and aristocratic surname, now used as a first name. The extremely prolific British composer Sir Charles Stanford (1852-1924) is the best known bearer of this name.

STANLEY (Stan)
Originally a surname taken from an Anglo-Saxon place name meaning 'stony field'. It was first brought into use in the second half of the 19th century. It reached its zenith in the 1920s, and is still commonly found.

STEPHEN (Steve, Stevie, Steven, Steffan, Steafan, Stefan, Stephan, Stepan)
Comes from the Greek for 'garland' or 'crown' and was the name of several saints, including the first Christian martyr. It was common in the Middle Ages leading to surnames such as Stephens, Stevenson and Stimpson. Though it became neglected in the late 1800s, it made a comeback as one of the top favourites in the middle of the 20th century.

STERLING
Means 'star'. The name implying top quality was promoted this century by the actor Sterling Hayden.

STUART (Stewart, Stu, Stewie, Stew)
A famous Scottish clan name, originally meaning 'steward', or 'sty ward', the keeper of the animals. It was the name of the royal house of Scotland which gave us four kings of England as well as two queens. It was

brought into use as a first name towards the end of the 19th century, a time when many Scottish surnames became fashionable. Since then it has spread into general use and is no longer confined simply to those with Scottish affiliations. It became highly thought of in the last decade in Britain and Australia.

---------------------- **T** ----------------------

TALBOT

An aristocratic surname, now used as a first name.
Richard Talbot came to England with William the
Conqueror.

TARQUIN

The family name of the legendary line of early Roman
kings, seven in number. Lucius Tarquinius Superbus,
the seventh and last king of Rome, was sent, with his
family, into exile in 510 BC and a republic established.

TAYLOR

An occupational surname, now a first name bestowed
on both boys and girls.

TERRANCE (Terrance, Terrence, Terry)

Derives from a Roman clan name, Terentius, the origin
of which is not known. After 1900 it came into widespread use, and was especially popular in the middle of
this century. It is still quite common, but in recent years
the abbreviated form, **Terry**, which is often treated as
an independent name, has occurred more frequently.

THANE

From the Old English, meaning 'servant'. A thane held
land given by the king and ranked with an earl's son.
It was the title of a clan chief in Scotland. Used as a
first name since the 19th century.

THEOBALD

Means 'bold people'. Along with Tybalt, it is a form of
the ancient name Theobeald.

THEODORE (Theo, Teddy)
Derives from the Greek meaning 'God's gift'. There
were several saints of this name, including a 7th-century
archbishop of Canterbury. It was not in general use in
Britain until the 19th century, although it had appeared
occasionally since the 17th century and was quite
common on the European Continent.

THOMAS (Tomas, Tom, Tommie, Tommy)
Means 'twin' in Aramaic and was the name of one of
the disciples in the New Testament. It caught the public
imagination following the murder of Thomas à Becket
in the 12th century and has been one of the best known
boys' names ever since. Throughout the centuries it has
remained a favourite and is still a very common name.

THORNTON
Means 'village near thorns'. This place name became
a first name when it was given to the American
playwright Thornton Wilder (1897-1975).

TIMON
The hero of Shakespeare's *Timon of Athens* is a rich
Athenian so generous that he becomes penniless and
goes to live in a cave where he finds a pile of gold.

TIMOTHY (Tim, Timmy, Timmie)
Derived from the Greek Timotheos meaning 'honouring
God'. It was not in use in England until interest in
Biblical names revived in the 16th century, since when
it has remained in circulation. From about the middle
of the 20th century, Timothy has received considerable
attention and the name is still fairly common, especially
in its short form, **Tim.**

TITUS
Means 'sun' or 'day'. The Roman Emperor Titus Flavius Vespasianus (9-79 AD) began building the Coliseum in Rome.

TOBY (Tobias)
The English version of **Tobias**, from the Hebrew meaning 'the Lord is good', now used by young parents as an independent name.

TODD
Comes from the English meaning 'fox'. Most frequently used as a surname, this is now occurs as a personal name, especially in the United States and Canada. It has made little impact yet in Britain, where the surnames are not so readily absorbed.

TORQUIL
From the Old Norse, meaning 'Thor's cauldron'. It was brought to England by the Danes before the Norman Conquest.

TRAVIS, TRAVERS
May come from the French for 'crossroads' or from the English surname and are unusual names in Britain. They are far more frequently used in other English-speaking countries, especially Australia.

TRENT
A place name which is strictly speaking a surname, but has been used as a boys' name in recent years.

TREVOR (Trefor, Trev)
An anglicisation of the Welsh name **Trefor**, from *tref*,

'homestead', and *mawr*, 'great'. Once anglicised, the name spread swiftly outside Wales, becoming very popular in the middle of the 20th century, and is still quite common.

TRISTAN, TRISTRAM

Comes from the Celtic *Drystan*, from *drest* or *drust*, meaning 'tumult' or 'din'. It is thought to be associated with *triste*, the French word for 'sad'. Tristram has survived since the 12th century as a name for boys, though it has never been popular, and Tristan, famous from the legend of *Tristan* and *Isolde*, is just as likely to be used today.

TROY

Probably comes from a French place name meaning 'from the place of the people with curly hair'. For some time this has been a popular name in the United States. It is now also widespread in Australia, but in Britain it has been slow to take off.

TYRONE

Developed from the Irish place name meaning 'Owen's country' and publicised by the actor Tyrone Power. American parents took it up, then it caught the imagination of British parents and was used quite often in the 1960s.

U

ULRIC

From the Old English, meaning 'wolf power'. The name was mentioned in the Domesday Book and has been the name of three saints. The English St Ulric (*d* 1154) was a priest in Wiltshire who ended his life as a recluse at Haselbury.

URBAN

From the Latin, meaning 'of the town'. The Urban of the New Testament was greeted by St Paul in his letter to the Romans. Several early saints and eight popes have borne the name.

URIAH

Means 'my light is God'. A biblical name taken up during the Reformation, then made notorious by Charles Dickens' cunning villain, Uriah Heep, in *David Copperfield* (1849-50).

V

VALENTINE (Val)

Is derived from the Latin *valens* meaning 'strong' or
'healthy'. This was a Roman name, and that of a
3rd-century martyr. It has been in use in Britain since
the 13th century, and has also sometimes been applied
to girls. Today Valentine is almost always a boys' name.
Though it still appears periodically, it is now fairly
unusual.

VAN

Is from the Dutch meaning 'of' or 'from'. It is usually
seen as the prefix to a surname, but is occasionally used
as a short form of a name or, in the United States and
Canada, sometimes treated as an independent Christian
name.

VAUGHAN (Vaughn)

Was originally a Welsh surname meaning 'little' and
has been used as a first name since the end of the 19th
century. Usually a boys' name, it is occasionally used
for girls.

VERE

A French place name and aristocratic surname, used
as a first name since the 17th century.

VERNON (Vern)

Derives from a common French place name meaning
'alder tree' or 'springtime' which came to Britain as a
Norman surname. It was adopted as a personal name
in the 19th century and did well in the early 1900s.

VICTOR (Vic, Vick)
Means 'conqueror' in Latin and was the name of an early pope and several Christian martyrs. It has been used in England since the 13th century and became popular because of its similarity to Victoria.

VINCENT (Vince, Vinnie)
Stems from the Latin meaning 'conquering' and was made famous by St Vincent of Saragossa, a 3rd-century martyr. It was used in medieval England but went through a spell in the doldrums before being revived in the 19th century. Since then it has been in use consistently, though never a top favourite

VIVIAN
Derives from the Latin word *Vivianus* meaning 'alive'. Vivian, the usual spelling for a boys' name, dates from medieval times but is seldom used today.

WADE
An Anglo-Saxon place name meaning 'dweller by the ford' or 'river crossing'. Usually regarded as a surname, in recent years it has been adopted as a personal name, first in the United States and now in Britain.

WALLACE (Wally, Wal)
Means foreign' in Anglo-Saxon. A Scottish surname, it was first given as a Christian name in the 19th century. It has now spread beyond Scotland and, although not common, is still in general use.

WALTER (Wally, Walt)
Taken from two Old German words, *vald* meaning 'rule' and *harja* meaning 'folk'. It came to England with the Normal Conquest and was common enough to give rise to surnames like Walters, Watson and Waters.

WARD
Derives from the surname meaning 'guardian' or 'watchman'. Though it was used as a first name in the 19th century, it disappeared from Britain for a time, coming back in recent years.

WARREN
Comes from the Old Germanic *Varin*, a folk name, meaning 'defender' or 'protection'. The Normans brought it to England where it became a surname but fell out of use as a first name for several hundred years. In the 19th century parents took it up again and it has been used quite often in recent years.

WARWICK

A place name, meaning 'farm beside a weir', used as a first name since the 19th century.

WAYNE

A surname meaning 'wagoner' or 'wagon-maker', from Old English, used as a given name in recent years, first in the United States and later in Britain.

WESLEY

Comes from an Anglo-Saxon place name meaning 'west meadow' which turned into a surname. Parents used it in honour of John Wesley, the 18th-century founder of the Methodists. It has never been very common in Britain, but it is better known in the United States.

WILBUR

Believed to be from Old German *wil*, 'will', and *burh*, 'defence'. This is an almost wholly American name, little known in Britain, where there are not even many surnames that are similar.

WILFRED (Wilf)

Comes from two Old English words, *will*, meaning 'will', and *frith*, meaning 'peace'. The name was in general use in the 19th century and was not uncommon at the beginning of the 20th century. It is little used in Britain today, however, possibly occurring more frequently in the United States.

WILLIAM (Bill, Billy, Will, Willie, Wills)
Derives from two Old German words, *vilja*, meaning 'will' and *helma*, meaning 'helmet'. It became famous in Britain through William the Conqueror. Many surnames came from it, including Williams, Wilkes and Willis, and through the centuries it has been a top favourite. It seemed to be on the decline in the 1970s but since the birth of Prince William in 1982 it is coming back into fashion.

WILLOUGHBY
A place name, meaning 'farm beside the willow trees', and aristocratic surname, now used as a first name.

WINSTON
A place name; it may mean 'wine settlement', or possibly it is connected with an Anglo-Saxon name Winestan, 'friend stone'. The Churchill family first adopted it as a Christian name in the 17th century; the first Sir Winston Churchill's mother was a Sarah Winston. Until the 20th century it remained chiefly confined to members of the family.

WYNDHAM
Began life as an Anglo-Saxon place name meaning 'windy settlement', taken as a family name and, in the 1800s, as a first name. A well-known bearer was the author Wyndham Lewis.

WYNSTAN
Means 'stony battleground'. A popular name in the Midlands, after the 9th-century saint and king of Mercia. During the 20th century, it was given to the poet Wynstan Hugh Auden (1907-73).

X

XAVIER
Comes from the Arabic for 'bright' or 'shining'. It was a place name in the Basque region of Spain, and the surname of a 16th-century Spanish Jesuit, St Francis Xavier, who was renowned for his missionary work in Japan and India. It is sometimes used as a Christian name by Roman Catholics.

XERXES
Means 'King'. The name of the Persian king (519-465 BC) who defeated the Greeks at Thermopylaoe.

Y

YALE
A Welsh place name, meaning 'fertile upland', and surname. Now used as a first name.

YEHUDI
A Hebrew name meaning 'praise'; made famous by the violinist Yehudi Menuhin, but seldom used.

YULE
A Norse name whose origins are either a 12-day long heathen festival, or a winter month that began mid-November.

YVES
Means 'God's mercy'. The French form of the Welsh name **Evan**, from **John**.

ZACHARIAS, ZACHARY (Zak, Zacaria, Zach, Zachery, Zeke)
Comes from the Hebrew meaning 'God has remembered', or 'the Lord is renowned'. Today it is rarely found in Britain, but more often in the United States. The shorter form is better known.

GIRLS'
NAMES

A

ABBEY (Abbie, Abby) see **ABIGAIL**

ABIGAIL (Abbey, Abbie, Gail, Gale, Gayle)
From the Hebrew meaning 'father's joy'. With the
Reformation and the Puritans' preference for names
of Biblical origin, this name came into favour.

ADA
Its origins are uncertain: possibly an Old German name
meaning 'noble', or a shortened form of a name such as
Adela.

ADELAIDE
From the Old German, meaning 'nobility'.

**ADÈLE (Adelia, Adelina, Adell, Adelle, Adela,
Della)**
The French pet form of **Adelaide** meaning 'nobility'.

ADELINE (Adaline, Adelina, Edelin, Lina)
Means 'noble'.

ADRIANA see **ADRIENNE**

ADRIENNE (Adria, Adrianne, Adriene)
The French feminine form of Adrian which proved
far more popular than **Adriana**.

AGATHA (Aggie)
From the Greek 'good'. St Agatha was a martyr in the
third century who is looked on as a protector against
fire.

AGNES (Aggie, Anis, Annice, Nancy, Nessie, Nesta)
From the Greek meaning 'pure' or 'chaste'.

AILEEN see **EILEEN**

AILSA
The Ailsa Craig is an island rock in the Firth of Clyde on the west coast of Scotland. Originally bestowed by Scottish parents on their daughters, the name is now rarely used.

AIMÉE see **AMY**

ALANA (Alanna, Alaine, Aline)
Feminine form of Alan, meaning 'peaceful harmony'.

ALBERTA (Albertine)
Feminine version of Albert, from the German meaning 'noble and bright'.

ALESSANDRA (Alessia, Sandra)
The Italian spelling of the feminine version of Alexander meaning 'defender'.

ALETHEA
From an ancient Greek word meaning 'truth'.

ALEXANDRA (Alex, Alexa, Alexandria, Alexandrina, Alexei, Alexina, Alix, Sacha, Sandra, Zandra)
A female and mainly Russian version of Alexander, meaning 'defender and protector of mankind'.

ALEXIS (Alex)
From the Greek meaning 'helper' or 'defender'. The name began as a boys' name, but is now more used for girls.

ALFREDA (Freda, Freddy)
Meaning 'intelligent and wise advice'.

ALICE (Alicia, Alise, Alisha, Alison, Alissa, Alix, Alyce, Alys, Alyse, Elissa, Lycia)
Derived from the Old German '*adalheidis*', meaning 'noble one', an ancient title for German princesses.

ALICIA see ALICE

ALINE
Originally used in the Middle Ages as a pet form of **Adeline**, it now stands as an independent name.

ALISON (Alise, Alisha, Alissa, Alix, Alyce, Alys, Alyse, Elissa, Lycia)
The Scots version of **Alice**. The true Gaelic form is **Ailis**, diminutive **Ailie**.

ALLEGRA
From Italy and means 'happy and cheerful'.

ALMA
Probably derived from the Latin word meaning 'kind' but may be from the Celtic for 'all good', the Hebrew for 'maiden' or the Spanish and Italian for 'soul' or 'spirit'. The term '*Alma Mater*', meaning foster-mother, was an affectionate nickname coined by the Romans for several of their favourite goddesses.

ALTHEA
Means 'healing, healthy'. An unusual Greek name which is also the botanical family name for the holly-hock.

AMABEL (Amabella, Mabel)
Means lovable.

AMANDA (Manda, Mandi, Mandy)
From the Latin, meaning 'lovable'.

AMARINDA
Means 'unfading', or 'everlasting'. A name poets give to an imaginary ever-flowering, ever-beautiful blossom.

AMBER
From the gemstone, this jewel name dates from the 19th century, however, amber beads have long been prized in Britain for their sweet smell as well as their beauty

AMBROSIA
Means 'food of life' and 'immortality'. The name for the food eaten by the mythological gods to perpetuate their immortality was later used for any food or smell fit for the gods.

AMELIA (Amalea, Ameline, Ammeline, Amy, Emelita)
Means 'industrious', 'earnest work'. A German name that is also popular in its anglicised form, **Emily**.

AMERY
Means 'hard-working in power'. Originally a German name, Almeric, it was introduced to Britain by the Normans.

AMORETTE
Means 'little love', 'sweetheart'. One of several names made up by writers to describe a character.

AMY (Amey, Aimée, Amie)
Derives from the Old French and means 'loved'. This name has been used in Britain since the Middle Ages, becoming especially popular since the 19th century.

ANASTASIA (Ana, Nastasya, Nastaya, Stacey, Stacy, Tasia)
From the Greek for 'resurrection'.

ANDREA (Aindrea, Andra, Andrée, Andria, Andrianna, Andrina, Drena, Rena)
Probably derived from **Aindrea**, the Gaelic form of Andrew meaning 'manly'.

ANGELA (Angel, Angelica, Angelina, Angelique, Angie, Anjela)
Stems from the Greek meaning 'messenger' or 'bringer of good tidings', and began as the feminine form of the boys' name Angel, which has now disappeared.

ANGELICA
'Angelic'. A name implying angel-like perfection.

ANGHARAD
A Welsh name meaning 'very much loved'.

ANITA (Nita)
A Spanish form of **Anne**, 'meaning favoured by God', 'fortunate'.

ANNA (Ana, Annah)
The Greek version of **Hannah** meaning 'grace', this name has been popular throughout time.

ANN(E) (Anice, Anina, Anita, Annette, Nana, Nanette, Nanna)
Comes from the Hebrew name **Hannah**, meaning 'grace'. This was originally the French version, but has long been common in Britain.

ANNABEL (Anabel, Annabelle, Annabella, Mabel)
Another form of **Amabel**, which comes from Latin meaning 'lovable'. Also means 'fortune' and 'beautiful'.

ANNEMARIE
A linking of **Anne** and **Maria**. **Annamari** is a variation and both can be used with or without a hyphen between the two names.

ANNETTE see **ANN**

ANNUNCIATA
'Bringer of news'. Derived through its association with the Annunciation – when the angel from God told Mary she would give birth to Christ – this is an apt name for a Christmas baby.

ANTHEA (Thea)
From the Greek word meaning 'flowery'. It was one of the titles of the goddess Hera in ancient Greece.

ANTONIA (Antonette, Antonica, Tanya, Toni, Tonia, Tony, Tonya)
The feminine form of Anthony, meaning 'flowering' or 'flourishing'.

ANUSHKA (Anouska)
The Russian pet form of **Ann**, now used in Britain.

APHRODITE
'Created from foam or dust'. Born out of the sea's waves, Aphrodite, the Greek goddess of love and fertility, was the personification of grace, beauty and charm.

APRIL
The name of the month which means 'ready for the sun'. The use of this month as a first name, with its springtime association of new life, began only in the 20th century.

ARABELLA or **ARABELLE (Belle, Bella)**
The origins of this name are obscure. Possibly derived from the Latin *orabilis*, 'yielding to prayer'. First known in Scotland, appearing in different forms – **Arabel**, Orable and Orabell in the 13th century, and later as Arbell and Arbella.

ARIADNE (Ariana, Arianna)
Meaning 'most divine', originating in Greek mythology.

ARLENE (Arleen, Arline, Arlyne, Arlena)
Possibly derived from a Gaelic word meaning 'pledge' but its origins are obscure.

ARTEMESIA (Artemisa, Artimisia)
Comes from Artemis, Greek goddess of the moon,
animals and hunting, and lover of music.

ASHLEIGH (Ashley)
From the Old English, meaning 'ash wood'. A place
name and a surname, now used as a first name for both
girls and boys, although the spelling **Ashley** is usually
preferred for boys.

ATHENA (Athene)
From the Greek goddess of wisdom, civilisation and
household skills, and also from the city of Athens.

AUDREY (Audra, Audree, Audria)
Began as a pet form of Ethelreda, which came from
the Old English meaning 'noble strength'.

AUGUSTA (Augustina, Gusta)
Means 'venerable'. A royal favourite introduced from
the German language by the Hanoverians.

AURORA (Aurore, Ora)
From Latin meaning 'golden dawn'.

AVIS (Avice, Aveza)
A girls' name brought to Britain by the Normans
meaning 'refuge in war'.

AVRIL see **APRIL**
The French word for the month of April.

AZURA
The Italian for 'blue skies'.

B

BABETTE (Babetta)
A French name which is a diminutive form of
Elizabeth.

**BARBARA (Babs, Barbi, Barbie, Barbra, Barby,
Bobbie)**
From the Greek word meaning 'strange', or 'foreign'.

BEATRICE (Bea, Beattie, Beatty, Bee, Trixie)
From the Latin *Beatrix*, meaning 'bringer of blessings'.
Beatrix was the earlier form of the name.

BATHSHEBA (Bathshua, Sheba)
Comes from Hebrew and means 'seventh child' and
'daughter of vow', or 'fulfilment'.

BECKY
A contraction of **Rebecca**, but considered a name on
its own.

BELINDA (Bel, Belynda, Linda, Lindy)
Linked with the Old German word for 'serpent' but
its origin is uncertain. Most likely to mean 'beautiful
snake'. In ancient Scandinavia, snakes symbolised
wisdom and immortality.

BELLA (Bel, Belle)
The Italian for 'beautiful' and the usual short form
of **Isabella** and **Arabella**. This name also means
'beautiful' in French.

BERNICE (Berenice, Bernie)
From the Greek meaning 'bringer of victory'.

BERNADETTE (Bernadine, Bernadot, Bernetta, Bernette, Bernie, Berny)
This is the French feminine form of Bernard meaning 'bear-like bravery'.

BERTHA (Bert, Bertina)
Means 'bright'.

BERYL
Comes originally from the Sanskrit name for a precious stone. It is an ancient word meaning a jewel with the qualities of clarity, preciousness and the power to bring good luck.

BESS (Bessie) see **ELIZABETH**

BETH (Beathag, Bethia)
A shortened form not only of **Elizabeth** but also the Old Hebrew name **Bethia,** meaning 'breath of life'.

BETHANY (Bethanie)
A Hebrew name meaning 'worshipper of God', which has become very popular recently.

BETTINA (Bettine)
A derivation of **Elizabeth,** occurring as a name in its own right.

BETTY (Bettie, Bette)
A form of **Elizabeth,** long accepted as an individual name.

118

BEVERLEY (Bev, Beverly)
From a place name meaning 'beaver stream'.

BIANCA (Biancha, Blanca, Blanche, Blandina)
From the Italian word for 'white' implying purity.

BILLIE
An old English name meaning 'determined', which is also a female form of William.

BLANCHE
Comes from the French word for 'white'.

BLITHE
Means 'gentle', 'mild'.

BONITA (Bonnie, Bonny)
Comes from the Latin for 'good' and the Spanish for 'pretty'.

BONNIE
A Scottish name meaning 'good', 'beautiful'.

BRENDA
Comes from the Old Norse word for 'sword'. It is also regarded as the feminine form of Brendan.

BRIDGET (Biddy, Birgitta, Bridie, Bridgette, Bridgid, Brigid, Brigit, Brit)
Comes from the Celtic for 'the high one' or 'the august one'. The name also belongs to the Celtic goddess of fire, light and poetry

BRIONY (Bryony)
An attractive plant name.

BRONWEN (Bronwyn)
Means 'white breast' in Welsh and is often used as
Bronwyn.

BROOKE
Means 'reward', 'pleasure'. An Old English word which
was adopted as a surname before it became a first name
for both sexes.

BUNTY
A pet name coined from a stage production at the
beginning of the 20th century. Also means 'little rabbit',
'bunny'.

C

CAITLIN
Means 'pure'. The Irish and Welsh form of **Catherine**.
As **Kathleen,** it reached Britain last century.

CALANTHA
Greek origins and means 'as beautiful as the flowers'.

CALISTA
Also Greek in origin and means 'fairer than all other
women'.

CAMILLA (Cammie, Camille, Millie, Milly)
Means 'witness at a ritual'. The name of the goddess
Diana's noble attendant in Roman mythology, it has
been popular since the 19th century, together with
the French form, **Camille**.

CANDACE (Candice, Candy)
Derived from the title of Ethiopian queens, it has
occurred occasionally in Britain since the 17th century,
but at the present time is better known in the United
States and Canada. **Candy** is the pet form.

CANDIDA
Means 'white hot'. A popular Roman name but hardly
found in Britain until the 20th century, encouraged by
the gentle heroine of Shaw's *Candida* (1898).

CARA (Kara, Carina)
Derived from Latin meaning 'dear', and 'friend' from
Celtic. This name is coming into fashion, especially in
the United States where it is spelt **Kara**.

CARLA (Karla, Carly, Karly)
Is the feminine version of Carl or Carlo, which became popular with American parents long before its use spread to Britain. **Carly** is a modern variation. Singer Carly Simon has made the variation popular.

CARLY (Karly) see CARLA

CARMEL
From the Hebrew meaning 'garden'.

CARMEN (Carmine, Charmain)
Means 'song' in Latin, and is familiar from the name of the heroine of Bizet's opera.

CAROL (Caryl, Carroll, Carole)
Is a form of Charles, and can be used as a boys' name though is usually given to a girl. The name has been constantly popular in recent times, and is now best associated with Christmas songs.

CAROLINE (Carolyne, Carolyn, Karolyn, Carolina)
Began as the feminine of Carlo, the Italian version of Charles. Meaning 'woman' or 'housewife', the name came to Britain in the 18th century with George II's bride and was instantly fashionable. It is still popular today.

CARRIE
An abbreviated form of **Carol** or **Caroline**. It has become popular as a name in its own right.

CARY (Carey)
The origins of this name seem uncertain. It may be
from an English place name Carew meaning 'fort', or
come from the Welsh, meaning 'dweller in a castle',
or possibly, as one authority suggests, from the Latin
'dear'. This is a surname which has occasionally been
adopted in recent times as a Christian name.

CASSANDARA (Cassandra, Cassie, Cass)
Derives from the Greek for 'helper of men', and is one
of the famous names of mythology, belonging to the
prophetess who foretold the fall of Troy. It is an old-
established name in Britain, most often used in the
17th century.

**CATHERINE (Cathryn, Catherina, Catrine,
Cathy, Kate, Katie)**
Originating from the Greek word meaning 'pure' it was
the name of a 4th-century martyr, St Catherine, who
was tortured on a spiked wheel (hence the name given
to wheel-shaped fireworks), and has been popular as an
English given name for 800 years. **Catherine** is the
favourite spelling, though the older forms are
Katherine or **Katharine. Cathleen** or **Kathleen** is
the Irish version, **Catriona** the Scottish and **Catrin**
the Welsh.

CATRIONA
A Scottish variant of **Catherine** and the title of a novel
by Robert Louis Stevenson. It is still very popular in
Scotland.

CECILA (Cecilia, Cicely, Sisley, Celia)
Stems from the Latin and means 'heavenly'. The early
spelling was Caelia, the form used in Ancient Rome.
The name was popular here in Britain in the 18th
and 19th centuries, along with **Cecilia**.

CECILIA see **CECILA**

CECILE
The French form of **Cecilia,** is sometimes used as
an abbreviation but also chosen occasionally as an
independent name.

CERYS
From the Welsh, meaning 'to love'.

CHANTAL (Chantelle)
A French girls' name which is occasionally borrowed
in English-speaking countries, and derived from the
word for 'song'. Not surprisingly, in view of the French-
speaking population, it is among the most popular
names in Canada.

CHARITY (Cherry)
One of the many 'virtue' names favoured by the
Puritans in the 17th century.

CHARLENE
A feminine version of Charles, in use since the 1950s.

**CHARLOTTE (Carlotta, Lotty, Lottie, Lolita,
Charleen, Charlie)**
The French and English form of **Carlotta,** a feminine
version of Carlo, the Italian for Charles. George IV's

daughter was named Charlotte, and it remained a favourite in Victorian times. Recently it has been revived and is rising rapidly in popularity.

CHELSEA (Chelsie)
This famous area of west London meaning 'a landing place for limestone' is now popular as a girls' name.

CHER
Comes from the French and means 'dearly loved'. It has grown in popularity recently due to the fame of the actress and singer, Cher.

CHERRY
Cherry began as a pet form of **Charity**, which had been popular with the 17th-century Puritans. It came into its own as an independent name along with the flower names favoured by the Victorians. Although not common it is still in regular use.

CHERYL (Cheryll, Cheralyn, Cherillynn, Cheryle, Sheral, Sherilyn)
A modern name which comes from the Welsh word for 'love' and has been well used by parents in English-speaking countries in recent years.

CHLOE (Cloe, Clea)
Derives from the Greek word meaning 'a tender budding plant', and in the past was always more popular with poets than with parents. However, like many of the old names, after being out of fashion for some time, it has become increasingly popular.

CHRISTABEL (Christabelle, Christobel, Christabella, Chris, Chrissie, Christy)
Means 'fair follower of Christ' and comes from a combination of Greek and Latin. It occurred in various forms from the Middle Ages onwards, becoming better known after Coleridge's poem of that name was published in 1816.

CHRISTINA (Cristine, Chris, Chrissy, Christy)
Stems from the Latin for 'follower of Christ', the name was first known in Italy from the 3rd-century Roman saint, St Christina. **Christine** reached a peak of popularity around 1950, and **Christina** is a favourite in the United States. The Scandinavian forms **Kirsten** or **Kristen** are occasionally borrowed in English-speaking countries.

CHRISTINE see **CHRISTINA**

CHRISTY (Christie)
Irish contraction of Christopher, stemming originally from the Latin, meaning 'fair follower of Christ'. It is also an abbreviation for **Christine** or **Christina**, but it may also be treated as an independent girls' name, especially in the United States.

CICELY (Sisley)
From the Latin meaning 'heavenly', this form of **Cecilia,** was particularly common before the 18th century. It was also sometimes rendered as **Sisley**. It is not a very widespread name at the present time. **Cissie** is an abbreviated form which is now regarded as rather old-fashioned.

CINDY
Is an abbreviation of **Lucinda** or **Cynthia** which has
become popular as a name on its own.

CLAIRE (Clare, Clara, Klara)
Derives from the Latin word meaning 'bright' or 'clear'
and has been used regularly for around 700 years.
Claire is the modern spelling and **Clara** was popular
in Victorian times.

CLARISSA
Replaced the Latin name Clarice and became well-liked
after the publication of a novel of the same name in
1748 by Samuel Richardson.

CLAUDETTE (Claudine)
Both are French feminine forms of Claudius, which
came from the Latin for 'lame'.

CLAUDIA
A feminine form of Claud, dating from Roman times
and mentioned in St Paul's Second Epistle to Timothy.

CLEO
Derived from the Greek, meaning 'fame and glory'.
Though strictly speaking this is the abbreviated form
of Cleopatra, it has in recent years occurred as an
independent name.

COLETTE
A shortened form for **Nicolette,** a French name which
came to Britain in the 1940s, following the success of
Gigi and other novels by the French writer Sidonie
Gabrielle Colette, known simply as Colette.

COLLEEN
Comes from the Irish for 'girl', and is now found more
in the United States than in Ireland.

CONNIE
A shortened form of **Constance**, which also appears as
a separate name, especially in the United States.

CONSTANCE (Constancy, Constantia, Connie)
Its descent can be traced from the Latin word meaning
'constancy'. It has been used in Britain in various forms
for hundreds of years: Custance in the Middle Ages,
Constancy in the 17th century and **Constantia** in
Victorian times.

CORA
Possibly from the Greek word meaning 'maiden', or
'girl'. It has been in use only since the 19th century,
and then chiefly in the United States.

CORAL (Coralie)
A jewel name, possibly derived from **Cora**.

CORDELIA
Means 'heart'. The Celtic name given to King Lear's
third and only loving daughter in Shakespeare's tragedy,
is probably derived from a German martyr named
Cordula.

CORINNA (Corinne)
From the Greek word meaning 'girl'. A diminutive form
of **Cora** and the name of a Greek poetess, it is believed
to date back to the 5th century BC. It was adopted by
Robert Herrick and other poets of the 17th and 18th

centuries and has been in steady use by parents ever
since, especially in its French form **Corinne**.

COURTNEY
A French place name. This surname has been used
occasionally in recent years as a Christian name for
both sexes.

CRESSIDA
A name of classical origin, from the Greek word
meaning 'gold'.

CRYSTAL (Chrystal, Christel)
Meaning 'ice', this Greek word came to be used for a
hard, brilliant rock, and was therefore a popular
Edwardian jewel name. It is also sometimes regarded
as a Scottish feminine version of Christopher.

CYNTHIA
A title of the Greek goddess of the moon, Artemis, 'of
Mount Cynthus'.

D

DAISY
Of all the flower names, this became one of the most popular at the end of the 19th century. Henry James used it in his celebrated story *Daisy Miller* in 1879. Originally a direct translation of the French girls' name **Marguerite**.

DANA
Dana comes from the name of the Celtic goddess of fertility and has been used for both girls and boys, especially in the United States.

DANIELLE (Daniele, Daniela, Daniella)
The French female form of Daniel. The increasing popularity of this name reflects the rising success of its male counterpart.

DAPHNE
Daphne means 'bay' or 'laurel' in Greek and was the name of a nymph loved by Apollo who was turned into a bush by the gods as she ran away from him. It appeared in Britain only at the end of the 19th century and was kept in the public eye by author Daphne du Maurier. Nick names are **Daff** and **Daffy**.

DARA
From the Hebrew, meaning 'pearl of wisdom'. Originally a male name featured in the Old Testament, it is used as a girls' name in modern times.

DARCY (Darcey)
Originally a surname, D'Arcy came from a French
place name, and was brought to England with the
Norman Conquest.

DARIA
The feminine form of Darius, one of seven Persian
chiefs, who invaded Greece, being defeated at the
battle of Marathon in 490 BC.

DARRYL
Generally considered a male name, but occasionally
bestowed on girls.

DAVINA (Davida, Davita, Devina, Vita)
From the Hebrew meaning 'darling'. This Scottish
feminine form of David, which dates from the 17th
century, has tended to oust the less popular **Davida.**

DAWN
An English translation of the old-established word
aurora, the Latin name for 'dawn'.

DEANNA
A variant of **Diana**, popularised in the 1940s by the
film actress, Deanna Durbin, and still fairly common.

DEANNE
Another form of **Diane**, the French version of **Diana**.
The use of the 'e' in place of the 'i' in the spelling
emphasises the correct French pronunciation.

DEBBIE
An abbreviated form of **Deborah** which recently seems to have been accepted as an independent name.

DEBORAH (Debora, Debra, Debbie)
Derives from the Hebrew, meaning 'bee'. The name of the Old Testament prophetess was particularly favoured by the Puritans of the 17th century, and has been used ever since.

DEE
Originated as a pet name for anyone whose names began with 'D' but is now used as a first name in its own right, particularly for girls, though it can be a boys' name.

DEENA (Dena, Dina)
Derives from the Old English, meaning 'valley'. This was considered to be the feminine version of Dean and has been used since the 1950s.

DEIRDRE
The origins are doubtful: possibly Old Celtic, 'the raging one', or Gaelic, 'the broken hearted'.

DELIA
Delia is another name for the Greek moon goddess Artemis, and was a favourite of 17th-century poets.

DELLA
Originally a variation of **Adèle**, but has become better known in its own right.

DELYS (Delise, Delissa)
Possibly comes from an old Latin first name meaning 'delight', though its exact origins have never been fully discovered.

DENISE (Denyse, Denice)
A French name, popular in the Middle Ages and back in favour during the 20th century.

DESDEMONA
The tragic heroine in Shakespeare's *Othello*. The name is a beautiful one but not commonly used.

DIANA (Diane, Dianna, Didi, Diona)
Latin name of the goddess of the moon, equivalent to the Greek goddess Artemis. She is also regarded as the goddess of the hunt. The name was first used in France as **Diane**, and adopted in England in the late 16th century in the form of **Diana**.

DIANE see DIANA

DIONNE (Dione, Diona)
In Greek mythology, Dione was a consort of the god Zeus and the mother of Aphrodite. The name has recently been brought back into the limelight.

DILYS
A Welsh name used in Wales and England since the mid 19th century, meaning 'sincere'.

DINAH
Dinah is an ancient Biblical name, meaning 'judged'. It is not a variant of Diana.

DODIE (Dodi)

A pet form of **Dorothy** or **Dorothea**, it is occasionally found as an independent name.

DOLORES (Lola, Lolita)

Comes from a Spanish name used as a short form for Maria de los Dolores, 'Mary of the sorrows', one of the titles of the Virgin Mary.

DOMINIQUE

French feminine version of Dominic, stemming from the Latin word meaning 'belonging to the Lord'.

DONNA (Maddona)

Originates from the Italian for 'lady', implying a woman worthy of respect. **Madonna** is a variant meaning 'my lady'.

DORA

Originally a familiar form of **Dorothy**, but by the 19th century it had come to be known as an independent name, a fashion initiated by the poet William Wordsworth early in the century when he christened his daughter.

DORCAS

Derives from the Greek, meaning 'gazelle'. In the New Testament, Dorcas is the Greek translation of the Aramaic name, **Tabitha**.

DOREEN

This is possibly a diminutive of **Dorothy.** It was first used at the end of the 19th century, and became very popular in Britain before the Second World War.

DORIS
A name from Greek mythology, meaning 'of the sea', which was also used by the Romans. Although there is no record of its earlier use in Britain, it suddenly leapt to popularity at the end of the 19th century.

DOROTHY (Dorothea, Dollie, Dot, Dotty, Dora)
From the Greek meaning 'gift of God'.

DRUSILLA
Derives from the family name of an Ancient Roman clan, and is a diminutive feminine form.

DULCIE
A modern name stemming from Latin and meaning 'sweet'.

E

EARTHA
Comes from Old English and means 'of the Earth'. It has been revived in recent years due to the fame of singer and TV personality Eartha Kitt.

EBONY
Derived from ebony wood. A name implying strength, value and durability.

EDITH (Edie, Eda, Ede)
Means 'successful in war'. A royal Anglo-Saxon name that survived the Norman Conquest and became one of the most popular names in the 1880s.

EDNA
Appearing in the Apocrypha it is assumed by some to be from the Hebrew word meaning 'rejuvenation'.

EDWINA (Edwena, Edwyna)
This is the female form of Edwin and has the meaning 'prosperous friend'.

EILEEN (Aileen, Eilean, Eilleen, Ilene)
Derives from the Celtic names Eibhlin and Aibhlin being a form of Eve, meaning 'life-giving'.

EIRWEN
From the Welsh, meaning 'golden-fair', used since the early years of the 20th century.

ELAINE
Means 'the bright one' and is an old French form of
Helen.

ELEANOR (Elinor, Ellen, Leonora, Nora)
Again, these all derive from an old French version of
Helen, meaning 'the bright one'.

ELISA (Eliza)
One of the many variations of **Elizabeth**, often regarded
as an independent name, and has been much used by
poets.

**ELIZABETH (Elisabeth, Elisavet, Elsa, Elspeth,
Bess, Beth, Bettina, Betsy, Lisa, Liza, Lizette,
Lisbet, Libby, Isabel)**
A royal name of universal popularity derived from the
Hebrew Elisheba meaning 'oath of God'.

ELLA
Norman French, originating from the Old German
name Aila, meaning 'all'.

ELLEN
An early English form of **Helen**, though it has for a
long time been recognised as an independent name,
it is also used as a form of **Eleanor**.

ELLIE
A pet form of **Eleanor**, which is now used independently.

ELMA
An abbreviation of Guilielma, the Italian feminine form of William.

ELSA (Ailsa)
Stems from two Old German words meaning 'noble maiden'.

ELSIE
One of the shortened forms of **Elizabeth** and a name in its own right. It went through a phase of great popularity around 1900.

ELSPETH
A Scottish derivative of **Elizabeth**, which has been in use since the 19th century.

ELVIRA
A Spanish name meaning 'wise advice'.

ELYSIA
From the Greek, meaning 'blissful'. In Greek mythology *Elysium* was the abode of the blessed dead.

EMERALD
Originating from the gem stone, this was another of the 'jewel' names so favoured by the Victorians.

EMILY (Emilie, Amelia, Emilia, Milly)
Together with **Amelia**, stems from an Old German word meaning 'hard-working'.

EMMA (Emaline)
Originates from Old German meaning 'universal'
or 'all-embracing'.

ENID
A Welsh name meaning 'life'.

ERICA (Erika)
The feminine form of Eric, it is however, also the
English translation of the Latin name for heather.

ERIN
From the Gaelic meaning 'western isle', a poetic name
which only recently appeared as a first name.

ERNESTINE
The feminine form of Ernest, which was occasionally
used in the 19th century. It is still to be found in the
United States.

ESME
Originates from the Latin 'esteemed' and was originally
a boys' name used in Scotland, but is now more likely
to be given to girls.

ESMERALDA
Derives from the Spanish for 'Emerald'.

ESTELLE (Estel, Estella, Stella)
Originates from Old French and means 'star'.

ESTHER (Etty, Hester, Hetty, Tessa)
Appearing in the Old Testament, this name comes from
the Persian, meaning 'star'.

ETHEL

From the Anglo-Saxon word meaning 'noble'.

EUGENIE

Originally from the Greek, meaning 'noble', this is the female French form of Eugene.

EUNICE (Younice)

Stems from the Greek, meaning 'happy victory'.

EUSTACIA

A feminine form of Eustace which has recently become very popular.

EVE (Eva, Ava, Evalina, Eveline, Evita, Aveline, Evonne, Zoe)

From the Hebrew meaning 'life-giving'. As the name of the first woman and mother in the Bible, it was believed to bring longevity.

EVELYN

Means 'hazelnut', and is associated with the Celtic fruit of wisdom.

F

FAITH
One of the 'virtue' names, introduced by the Puritans, at the time of the Reformation.

FANNY
An abbreviation of **Frances**, and occasionally used as an independent name, gaining popularity in the 1950s.

FAUSTINA
Stems from the Latin and means 'good luck'.

FAY (Faye)
Possibly from the Old English word *fay* meaning 'faith', or perhaps derived from the Old French *fae*, meaning 'fairy'.

FELICITY (Felicia, Felice)
The most usual form of the female equivalent of Felix, taken from the Latin *felicitas* meaning 'happiness'. Pet forms include **Fee** and **Flic**.

FENELLA (Finola)
Gaelic in origin and means 'white shoulders'.

FERN
Derives from the plant of the same name and is more commonly used in the United States than it is in Britain.

FIONA
Originates from Gaelic meaning 'fair white'.

FLAVIA (Flavie)
A Roman name meaning 'blonde', and taken up by the French as **Flavie**.

FLEUR
Derives from the French meaning 'flower'.

FLORA (Flore, Florella, Floris)
Comes from the Latin for 'flowers', and is the name of a Jacobite heroine, Flora Macdonald.

FLORENCE (Florrie, Flo, Flossie)
Derives from the Latin for 'blooming' and became especially popular as a girls' name with the fame of Florence Nightingale.

FRANCES (Fanny, Francie, Franke, Fran)
Stems from the Latin word meaning 'Frenchman' also means 'free' in Germanic and Old French.

FRANCESCA
The original Italian feminine form of Francis, often borrowed in English-speaking countries.

FREDA (Elfrieda, Frida, Frieda)
Originally an abbreviation of **Winifred**, and of **Frederica**, it has long been used as a separate name.

FREDERICA
A female form of Frederick, meaning 'gentle ruler'.

FREYA (Freja)
The Norse goddess of love and fertility, also meaning 'noble lady'.

GABRIELLA (Gabrielle, Gabby, Gabi)
The Italian female form of Gabriel, meaning 'God's heroine'.

GABRIELLE see **GABRIELLA**

GAIL (Gayle)
A modern addition to British names and originally a diminutive of **Abigail** meaning 'a father's joy'.

GARNET
Originates from the precious stone of the same name.

GAY (Gaye)
Means 'lively' in French, but could come from the Greek meaning 'earth goddess'.

GAYNOR (Gayner, Gaenor)
Developed from **Guenevere**, the name of King Arthur's wife who fell in love with Lancelot. It means 'fair lady'.

GEMMA (Jemma)
Italian for 'gem'. This name honouring St Gemma of Galgani is now one of the top 50 British names.

GENEVIEVE
Genevieve is a French name but its origins and meaning are uncertain. The 5th-century St Genevieve is the patron saint of Paris, so the name has always been popular with French families. In Britain it is still an unusual name.

GEORGETTE
A French form of a feminine version of George, sometimes borrowed in English-speaking areas to provide an unusual Christian name.

GEORGIANA (Georgina, Gina, Georgia, Georgie)
The feminine form of George meaning 'labourer', popular in the 18th century when George first became fashionable. After the 19th century **Georgina** was the version more often seen and it is still in general use.

GERALDINE
The feminine form of Gerald meaning 'ruler by spear'.

GERTRUDE (Gertie, Gerda, Trudie, Trudy, Trudi)
Derives from the Old German meaning 'spear strength'. The 7th-century St Gertrude of Belgium was the patron saint of travellers.

GILLIAN (Gillianne, Gilly, Jilly, Gill, Jill)
Originally another form of **Juliana**, the feminine form of Julian, supposed to mean 'downy'. It was common in the Middle Ages, then came back into fashion in the 20th century.

GINA
Originally the pet form of names like **Regina** and **Georgina**, but has become a personal name in its own right, during the 20th century.

GINGER
A pet name for **Virginia**, but can also be used descriptively to mean 'red-haired'.

GINNY see **VIRGINIA**

GISELLE
From German meaning 'a pledge'. It was made popular by the success of the well-loved and timeless ballet of the same name.

GLADYS
A Welsh name, meaning 'ruler over territory', which was not used outside Wales until nearly the end of the 19th century. **Glad** is a pet form.

GLENDA
Derived from Wales meaning 'holy', 'goodness'.

GLENNIS see **GLYNIS**

GLORIA (Gloriana)
Means 'glory' in Latin, the name was originally Gloriosa, then **Gloriana** to honour Elizabeth I.

GLYNIS
The feminine version of Glyn, comes from the Welsh meaning 'little valley'.

GOLDA (Goldie)
Derived from the Ango-Saxon 'gold' and has been in use for 800 years, sometimes in the form **Goldie**.

GRACE
One of the 'virtue' names favoured by the Puritans, originating from the Latin *gratia*.

GRISELDA (Grizelda, Grizzle, Zelda)
Means 'grey warrior'. A German name still asssociated with the exemplary, patient wife in Giovanni Boccaccio's *Decameron* (1348-53), later retold by Chaucer in *The Clerk's Tale*.

GUENEVERE (Guinevere, Gwenhwyvar)
Welsh for 'fair and yielding'. The old Cornish version **Jenifer** gave rise to the modern **Jennifer**. **Gwinny** is often used as a pet name.

GWEN
Welsh in origin it is the feminine form of Gwyn, meaning 'white, fair'. It is also an abbreviation of **Gwendolen**, but is often given as an independent name.

GWENDOLEN (Gwendolen, Gwendoline, Gwendolyn, Gwenda, Gwen)
A long established Welsh name meaning 'white'. **Gwendoline** was also the name of the Celtic moon goddess.

GWYNETH (Gwynyth, Gwynneth)
Another Welsh name, meaning 'blessed with happiness'. As Gwynedd, it is the Welsh name for North Wales. Short forms are **Gwyn** and **Gwinny**.

HANNAH (Hanna, Anna, Anne, Nana)
One of the oldest names, **Hannah** is from the Hebrew meaning 'God has favoured me'.

HARRIET (Harriot, Hattie, Hatty, Harrie, Ettie)
Evolved from **Harry**, a nickname for **Henrietta** meaning 'ruler at home'.

HAYLEY
A surname, adopted in recent years as a girls' Christian name, originally a place name meaning 'hay-meadow'.

HAZEL (Hazell, Hazelle)
One of the tree and flower names which were first taken up as personal names at the end of the 19th century. The ancient Hazel wand symbolised wisdom and protection.

HEATHER
Another of the flower names adopted at the end of the 19th century, which has been very successful, especially between 1950 and 1960.

HEBE
The Greek goddess of youth, daughter of Zeus and Hera.

HEIDI
From the German name Adelheid meaning 'nobility'.

HELEN (Helena, Lena, Nell, Nellie)

A name from which many others derive, Helen originates from Greek and means 'the bright one'. The name
became well known through St Helena, mother of the
Emperor Constantine, though it is with Helen of Troy,
'the face that launched a thousand ships', that this
name is always associated.

HENRIETTA (Henriette, Harriet, Harry, Hetty, Etty, Etta)

The feminine form of Henry meaning 'home ruler'
which came to Britain through the French wife of
Charles I; her name was Henriette Marie, but the
British called her Henrietta Maria.

HERMIONE (Hermia)

Originates from Hermes, the name of the messenger
of the gods in Greek mythology.

HESTER

An alternative spelling of **Esther**.

HETTY see ESTHER and HENRIETTA

HILARY (Hillary, Hilaire)

Derives from the Greek word for 'cheerful'. The name
was known in England from the 13th century, when it
was applied to both sexes. Today however, the name is
largely given to girls.

HILDA

Evolved from an Old German text denoting 'battle-
maid'. It was made famous by an Anglo-Saxon abbess
of Whitby, St Hilda.

HILDEGARD

A German name whose meaning is unclear, but the first part means 'battle'. The rest appears to be in dispute, 'spear', 'stronghold' or 'to know' being some of the meanings given by different authors.

HOLLY

A modern name taken from the name of the holly-tree and often used for girls born around Christmas time. It is the bright red berries of the tree that symbolise life, and give this name added meaning.

HONEY see HONOR

HONOR (Honour, Honoria, Honey)

Derives from the Latin for 'honour' or 'reputation'. Originally used as **Honoria**, but later favoured by the Puritans as one of the 'virtue' names.

HOPE

Another of the 'virtue' names which were particularly favoured by 17th-century Puritans, meaning 'optimistic wish'.

HORTENSE (Hortensia)

Hortense is the French form of a Latin family name which is occasionally borrowed by English parents for their daughters.

HYACINTH

Came into use in the late 19th century, when the 'flower' names were at the height of their popularity.

I

IANTHE
From the Greek, meaning 'violet flower', it was a name favoured by Romantic poets in the 19th century.

IDA
Stems from the Old German for 'a woman'.

ILA (Isla)
Originates from the French 'from the island' and the Anglo-Saxon, 'island dweller'.

ILLEANA (Ilona, Illeane)
Modern variants of **Eleanor**, and therefore another variant of **Helen**.

IMOGEN
Believed to be originally a misprint of Innogen, perhaps from Old Irish *ingen*, meaning 'daughter' or 'girl'. It was the name of the heroine in Shakespeare's *Cymbeline*, the play in which the misprint occurred.

INDIA
The country; originally from the Greek *indos*, meaning the river Indus. A name increasing in popularity in recent times.

INGRID (Inga, Inge, Inky)
Derives from the Old Norse name Ing, the god of fertility, and has always been popular in Scandinavia.

IOLE
A name from Greek mythology which was revived by the Victorians in the late 19th century.

IONA
Originates from the Greek, meaning 'violet-coloured stone', however, it is now associated with the Hebridean island. The name is very popular in Scotland.

IRA
Stems from Hebrew and means 'watcher'.

IRENE (Irena, Rena, Rene, Renie)
The gentle name for the Greek goddess of peace, this can be pronounced either as two syllables, or as a three syllable word.

IRIS
Means 'rainbow' in Greek, however, it was as the flower name that it first came to be used at the end of the 19th century, when such names came into fashion.

IRMA
German in origin, a short form of **Ermintrude** and the name of a Teuton god.

ISABELLA see ISABEL

ISABEL (Isabelle, Isobel, Isabella, Isa, Belle, Bella, Ibby)
Originally a variation of **Elizabeth** meaning 'oath of God', there are numerous spellings of the name, and many variations.

ISADORA
The feminine form of Isidore, a Greek name referring to Isis, the Egyptian goddess of the moon and fertility.

ISLA see **ILA**

ISOLDE
An ancient Celtic name meaning 'fair one'.

IVANNA
The feminine form of Ivan, meaning 'God is gracious'.

IVY
One of the plant names which came into use at the end of the 19th century. The name attained quite a high level of popularity during the first quarter of the 20th century.

J

JACINTA
Derives from the flower name **Hyacinth**.

JACKIE see **JACQUELINE**

JACQUELINE (Jacquelyn, Jacalyn, Jacquette, Jacquetta, Jacolyn, Jacqueline, Jackie, Jacky)
The feminine form of the French Jacques (James), has the meaning 'supplanter'.

JACQUETTA see **JACQUELINE**

JADE
Originates from the Eastern precious stone.

JAMIE
One of the abbreviated forms of James, it is now being chosen as a girls' name.

JANE (Jayne, Jinny, Janie, Janey)
One of the feminine forms of John deriving from the Hebrew, meaning 'God is gracious'. It was very popular until the mid-1800s, coming back into favour during the 20th century.

JANET (Jennet, Jannet, Janine, Jannette, Jenny)
Originally a diminutive of **Jane**, but long recognised as a separate name. It first evolved in Scotland from the French **Jeanette** and though it was always especially favoured there, it became widely popular in the middle of the 20th century, in all English-speaking countries.

JANICE (Janis)
A modern development of **Jane,** and one which became
very popular in the 1950s.

JANINE see **JANET**

JASMINE (Yasmine)
The Persian word for the sweet-smelling jasmine flowers
was fashionable with the Victorians, revived in the
1930s, and is still popular today.

JAYNE see **JANE**

JEAN (Jeanne, Jeanette, Jeanine)
Another of the names which originated with **Joanna,**
having evolved from the Old French Jehane. It was
regarded as one of the Scottish forms of **Jane,** but has
long been widespread in England and has lost any
particular association.

JEMIMA
Derives from the Hebrew for 'dove' and is the female
version of Benjamin. Pet names include **Jem, Jemmy**
and **Mima.**

JENNIE See **JENNIFER**

**JENNIFER (Jennie, Jenna, Jenny, Jen, Gaynor,
Ginevra)**
Jennifer began as a Cornish version of the name
Guenevere, meaning 'fair lady', and only spread
throughout the country in modern times.

JESSICA (Jessie, Jessye, Jess)
The feminine form of Jesse, meaning 'God beholds' in Hebrew. Its use as a Christian name seems to stem from Shakespeare's choice of it for *The Merchant of Venice*. Before that it had been regarded chiefly as a Jewish name.

JILL (Jilly)
A short form of **Gillian** which has been very successful in its own right.

JINNY see **JANE** and **VIRGINIA**

JOAN
Another feminine form of John, derived from **Joanna**. The name first came from France as Jhone or Johan in the 12th century, taking its present form by the 13th century, and predating both **Jane** and **Jean**.

JOANNA
The original feminine version of John meaning 'God is gracious', together with the French form **Joanne** they are both in the British top 50 names.

JOCASTA
In Greek legend, the mother and unwitting wife of Oedipus. She is the tragic heroine of many dramas. The name appears to have been first used by the Victorians.

JOCELINE (Jocelyn, Joscelyn)
'Of the Goths', a name referring to the German people, it was introduced by the Normans and given only to boys, until the 20th century.

JODIE (Jodi, Jody)
Means 'praise' and is a variation of **Judy**, the shortened form of **Judith**. The name is now gaining popularity in its own right.

JOELLE
The French female form of Joel, meaning 'God's willingness'.

JOLIE
Thought to be derived from **Julia**, though in recent times it has become a name in its own right.

JOSEPHINE (Josie, Joey, Jo, Fifine, Pepita, Pheeny)
The French feminine diminutive of Joseph, meaning 'may the Lord add'.

JOSIE see **JOSEPHINE**

JOY
A simple name meaning just what it says, dating back to the 12th century. After a period of neglect, it came back into favour in the first half of the 20th century.

JOYCE
Derives from the Celtic Jodoc, a 7th-century Breton saint. It was a medieval name for both sexes, appearing in many forms. The most common English version was Josse, and the name was often registered as Jocea or Jocosa. It was revived at the end of the 19th century, and is now mainly used for girls.

JUDITH (Judy, Judi, Jodie, Jody)
Judith is a very old name, meaning 'a Jewess' in Hebrew, however, it is only since the 17th century that the name has been widely used.

JUDY see **JUDITH**

JULIA (Juliana, Jillian, Jill, Gillian)
Feminine versions of the Latin name Julius, meaning 'downy'. It was much used by parents in the 18th century, but in modern times has been overtaken by the French form **Julie**.

JULIE see **JULIA**

JULIET (Juliette, Julietta)
Derives from the Italian name Guilietta, a diminutive of Guilia, from which we may take our **Julia**. Its popularity is due to the use Shakespeare made of it in the great tragic love story, *Romeo and Juliet*.

JUNE
As the name of the month it originates from the important Roman family, Junius, and from Juno, the mother of the Roman god of war, Mars.

JUSTINA (Justine)
Feminine forms of Justin, meaning 'just'. **Justine** the French form is now more popular than the long-established **Justina**, the name of a 4th-century martyr.

K

KARA
This is the preferred American spelling of **Cara**.

KAREN (Karena, Karin, Karon)
Meaning 'pure', this is Danish form of **Catherine** and came to Britain from the United States. It has been a modern favourite in both countries, with numerous variations.

KATE
A short form of **Katharine**, it was popular in the 16th and 17th centuries, returning to esteem in the 19th century. Since then it has remained a favourite form of **Katharine**, and an accepted name in its own right.

KATHARINE (Katherine, Kathy, Kitty, Katie, Katy)
Simply an alternative spelling for **Catherine**, but this is the form which has given rise to many variations.

KATHERINE see **CATHERINE**

KATHLEEN (Cathleen)
The Irish form of **Katherine**, extensively used in all English-speaking countries. It was very popular around the 1950s.

KATHY (Cathy)
Popular pet form of **Katherine**, especially liked in the United States.

KATIE (Katy)
This form of **Catherine**, meaning 'pure', is now in the British top 20 names.

KAY (Kaye)
Held to mean 'rejoice'. Although originally a nickname for any girl whose name began with a 'K', as well as a diminutive of **Karen** and **Katherine**, it has recently established itself as an independent name.

KELLY (Kayley, Kealy, Kellie, Kerley, Keeley)
A modern anglicised form taken from a Gaelic name Caelach, meaning 'warrior', it is now among the top 10 favourite names.

KERRY (Kerri, Kerrie)
Stems from the Irish county name, originally meaning 'dark'. Originally a mans' name, it is one of the new names introduced into general use in the last twenty-five years, which has become especially popular.

KIM
A short form of the name **Kimberley**, which originally derived from the Anglo-Saxon surname Kimball, meaning 'bold'. Although once a male name, it has come to be regarded largely as a girls' name.

KIMBERLEY (Kimberly, Kimberlee, Kimber)
The original form from which the name **Kim** was derived, this longer version tends to be preferred in the United States.

KIRSTEN (Kirstin, Kirsteen, Kirstyn, Kersteen)
Originally a Scandinavian form of **Christiana** or **Christine**, it is now regarded chiefly as a Scottish variant and means 'annointed'.

KIRSTY (Kirstie)
A shortened pet form of **Kirsten** which has become a favourite as an independent name.

KITTY see **KATHARINE**

KRISTINE see **CHRISTINA**
An alternative spelling of **Christine** common in the United States and Australia, but seldom seen in Britain.

KYLE
A Gaelic name used for both boys and girls, and means 'handsome'.

KYLIE (Kyly)
A girls' name meaning 'curl'. This name was used by the Australian Aborigines to describe a 'boomerang'; it is Australia's third favourite girls' name, helped by the popularity of the singer Kylie Minogue.

L

LANA
Lana is from the Greek for 'shining' and is occasionally used in the United States. The Irish **Alana** meaning 'my child', is a similar name more likely to be used in Britain.

LARA (Larah)
Originates from the Latin for 'famous'. As a first name, it caught the imagination of English-speaking parents following the spectacular 1960s film of Boris Pasternak's *Doctor Zhivago*.

LARISSA (Larisa)
Probably introduced into Britain from Russia, this name means 'playful'.

LAURA (Lora, Lauren, Laureen, Lauri, Laurel, Laurette, Lorraine, Lorna)
Derives from the Latin *laurus*, meaning 'laurel'. For the Romans the laurel-wreath was a symbol of outstanding achievement. There are many popular variations of the name.

LAUREN see **LAURA**

LAURI see **LAURA**

LAVENDER
The fragrant, pale mauve flowers made this an especially appealing Victorian flower name.

LAVINA (Lavinia, Vina)

A classical name, that of the second wife of Aeneas. It was adopted after the Renaissance and became quite popular.

LEAH

Derives from the Hebrew, meaning 'gazelle'. The Puritans of the 17th century began the use of the name in Britain.

LEANNA (Leana, Liana, Leanne, Leann, Lian)

Thought to derive from the French **Liane**, meaning 'climbing vine', or simply, a double-name combination of **Lee** and **Anne**, or **Lee** and **Anna**. The name is highly popular in Australia, and there is increasing interest in Britain.

LEANNE see LEANNA

LEE (Leigh)

Originally a surname from the Anglo-Saxon for 'meadow'. It was first used as a personal name by American parents, and has become popular in Britain. It is usually a boys' name but can also be used for girls, and is increasingly popular.

LEILA (Leilah, Lela, Lila)

Has its roots in a Persian name meaning 'dark-haired', also being the name of a heroine in Persian romance.

LENA

A German shortened form of **Helena**, but also recognised as an independent name which is sometimes used in English-speaking countries.

LEONORA (Nora)
A name which occurs in many languages and may be
a derivation of the name **Eleanor**. It was made popular
in England in the 19th century as the name of the
heroine in Beethoven's opera *Fidelio*.

LESLEY (Leslie)
Originally derived from an Aberdeenshire place name,
this is a Scottish surname, adopted as a personal name
around the end of the 19th century. It is used for both
sexes, **Lesley** being the feminine form while **Leslie**
usually remains the masculine.

LETITIA (Lettice)
From the Latin meaning 'full of joy' and 'happiness'.
Lettice is a variant and used to be common in Tudor
England.

LIBBY
A pet form of **Elizabeth** which is occasionally used
as a name in its own right.

LILIAN (Lillian, Liliana, Lilia, Lilias)
May have developed from a pet form of **Elizabeth,** or
from the name of the flowering lily. It made its biggest
impact around the beginning of the 20th century and is
often shortened to **Lil** or **Lily**, while Scottish parents
sometimes use **Lilias**.

LILY (Lilly, Lillie)
The bloom that symbolises 'purity'. This name was
widely used in the 19th century when other flower
names became fashionable. See also **Lilian**.

LINDA (Lynda, Lindy)
Deriving from the Old German word meaning 'serpent', it has Scandinavian associations with wisdom and immortality.

LINDSAY (Lindsey, Lynsey, Lindsay)
An ancient Scottish surname taken from a place name, 'Lindon's Isle'. In recent years it has been increasingly adopted as a girls' name outside Scotland. **Lindsey** tends to be the spelling form most favoured in England, **Lindsay** in Scotland.

LINNET (Lynnette, Linette, Lyn, Lynne)
A version of the Welsh name Eiluned, meaning 'icon', but also the name of the songbird with which the name is often associated.

LISA (Liza)
'God's oath'. A derivative of **Elizabeth**, now established as an independent name, and among the top 10 favourite girls' names.

LISE (Lisette)
Two other shortened forms of **Elizabeth**, from the French form, **Elise**, which are sometimes used independently.

LIZ (Lizzy, Lizzie)
A favourite shortened version of **Elizabeth**, which is still very popular.

LIZA
Another abbreviation of **Elizabeth**, it is more closely associated with its source than the similar name **Lisa**, which has taken on a life of its own.

LOIS
A more unusual biblical name from the Greek, meaning 'good' and 'worthy of desire'.

LOLA (Lolita)
Pet forms of the name **Dolores**, these are often used independently.

LORA
The older spelling of **Laura**, it is sometimes used in England and still appears as an alternative spelling form today.

LORETTA (Lauretta)
A well-used Roman Catholic name, possibly deriving from Our Lady of Loreto in Italy, or even from the name **Laura**.

LORI (Lorrie, Lory)
A pet form of Lorraine, this is increasingly being used as an independent name. **Lory** is also a brightly coloured Australian parrot, which dines on the nectar and pollen of flowers.

LORNA (Lorne, Lorena)
Thought to be derived from an Old English word meaning 'forsaken'. The name was used by R.D. Blackmore for his novel *Lorna Doone* (1869). Since then it has been in steady use as a personal name.

LORRAINE (Loraine, Lorayne)
Originates from a French place name, and was first used as a given name by Scottish parents. In the middle of the 20th century it was a favourite in both Britain and the United States.

LOTTIE (Lotty) see **CHARLOTTE**

LOUELLA
A combination of **Louise** and **Ella**.

LOUISA see **LOUISE**

LOUIE see **LOUISE**

LOUISE (Louisa, Louie, Eloise, Heloise, Lulu)
The French and feminine form of Louis meaning 'glorious in war', has always been popular. **Lou** is often used as a pet form.

LUCINDA (Cindy)
A poetic version of **Lucy** with the meaning 'shining out', fashionable in the 17th century. **Cindy** is the short form.

LUCRETIA
The Roman woman who committed suicide in shame after Tarquinius raped her, not the infamous Lucretia Borgia, gave this name its associations with virgin purity.

LUCY (Lucie, Lucia, Lucilla, Lucille, Lucile)
The Latin feminine version of Lucius meaning 'light'.
In early times the name was given to children born at
daybreak, however the name has continued to remain
popular throughout time.

LYDIA
Comes from the Greek, meaning 'woman of Lydia'.
Though it appears in the Bible, it only became widely
used in the middle of the 18th century, and has
survived ever since. The pet name is **Liddy**.

LYN (Lynn, Lynne)
Pet forms of the Welsh name Eiluned, they are also
short forms of **Lindsay** or **Linda**, as well as being
accepted as independent names.

LYNDA see **LINDA**

LYNSEY see **LINDSAY**

M

MABEL (Mabelle, Mable, Mabella)
Believed to have derived from the Old English name
Amabel, but may come from the French *ma belle*,
meaning 'my beautiful girl'.

**MADELEINE (Madeline, Madilyn, Magdalene,
Magdalena, Marla, Marleen, Marlene, Maddie,
Maddy)**
Stems from the Hebrew meaning 'woman of Magdala',
St Mary Magdalene was the patroness of penitents.
This original French form tends to be preferred to
the British version, **Madeline**.

MADGE see **MARGARET**

MADDISON (Madison)
Originally from the surname, meaning 'son of Maude'.
A modern first name for girls, especially popular in the
United States, after the fourth president, James Madison.

MAE
A pet form of **Margaret**, and an alternative spelling
of **May**.

MAEVE
An anglicised version of Meadhbh, a legendary Irish
warrior queen, and still a popular name in Ireland
today.

MAGGIE (Maggy) see **MARGARET**

MAIA (Maya)
From the Greek, meaning 'nurse'. The Romans also honoured an ancient divinity of Spring with this name. They offered sacrifices to her on the first day of May, naming the month after her.

MAIDA (Maidie)
Means 'unmarried girl'. This and **Maidie** enjoyed Victorian and Edwardian popularity, to be revived in the 1960s.

MAISIE
A Scottish short form of **Margaret**, used as a name in its own right, enjoying great popularity in the 1920s and 30s.

MAME (Mamie)
An American pet form of **Mary**, often treated as an independent name. It rarely appears in Britain.

MANDY
A modern short form of **Amanda** or **Miranda**, which is now recognised as an individual name.

MANON
A French diminutive of **Mary**, best known as the heroine of the operas *Manon Lescaut* (1893) by Puccini, and *Manon* (1884) by Massenet.

MARCELLA (Marcelle)
One of the female forms of Mark, this name is held to mean 'shining'.

MARCIA (Marsha, Marcie, Marcy)
Feminine form of the Latin name Marcius, a Roman clan name, originating possibly from Mars, the god of war, and representing the feminine form of Marcus. The name has been used over the past 100 years, although, it has always been more common in the United States than in Britain.

MARGARET (Margot, Magot, Madge, Megan, Meg, Maggie, Maggy, Margaretta, Margareta, Margherita, Margarita, Marguerite)
This extremely popular name, and all its subsequent variations stem from the Greek and mean 'pearl'. It is even suggested that it was originally Persian, meaning 'child of light'. It has long been a favourite of European royalty and remains an enduring name, especially popular in Scotland.

MARGERY (Marjorie, Marge, Margie)
Originally a form of **Margaret**, evolving from the French version **Marguerite**, but has been an independent name since early times.

MARGOT (Margo) see **MARGARET**

MARGUERITE
The French version of **Margaret**, and the direct English translation being 'daisy', helped ensure this name's popularity.

MARIA
The Latin form of **Mary**, widely used in Italy and Spain.

MARIANNE

A favourite derivative of **Marie** in France, where it symbolises France itself. In English-speaking countries it sometimes replaces **Marion**, and can also be interpreted as a 'double' name, **Mary Anne**, a style which was quite common in the 18th and 19th centuries.

MARIE (Marietta, Marielle)

The French form of **Mary** which in the present generation, has taken over as the popular form. Its pet form is **Mimi**.

MARIGOLD

A flower name meaning 'Mary's gold', that has remained popular, perhaps because **Mary** refers to the Virgin.

MARILYN (Maralyn, Marylyn, Marrilynne)

Thought to mean 'Mary's line', referring to decendants of the Virgin Mary. The name received great fame due to the actress Marilyn Monroe, making it a favourite name in 1950s Britain.

MARINA

From the Latin, meaning 'of the sea'. In Shakespeare's *Pericles*, Marina is the daughter of Thaisa and Pericles, called so 'for I was born at sea'.

MARION (Marian, Marianne)

A development from **Mary**, via the French form **Marie**, often used in medieval times and given a boost by the Robin Hood legends, with their heroine Maid Marian. Together with its variants, it has been frequently used by parents over the past 100 years.

MARLENE (Marlena)

A contraction of Mary Magdalene, for which **Marlena** was an abbreviation in parts of Europe in the late 19th century. Both names are still used.

MARSHA see MARCIA

MARTHA (Marty, Marti, Marta)

Derives from the Aramaic meaning 'lady'. Martha, the biblical figure who complained of her household chores to Jesus, is now patroness of housewives. The name has enjoyed some popularity in Britain since the 17th century, but is now more common in the United States.

MARTINA

The female form of the French name for Martin meaning 'warlike'. This name became especially popular in the 1950s.

MARTY see MARTHA

MARY (Marion, Marnie, Miriam, Maria, Marie, Maura, Maureen, May, Mia, Mimi, Minnie, Mira, Molly, Polly, Moira, Moyra, Mitzi, Mair)

Thought to derive from Hebrew, or possibly ancient Egyptian, 'beloved of Mane', the name of an early Egyptian god. There seems to be some doubt about the origins of Mary, one of the oldest names and the most significant in the Christian Church. **Miriam** is the oldest form known, though seems not to possess a clear meaning. The Virgin Mary, mother of Jesus Christ, inspired a cult so fervent that the name was sometimes considered too holy to use. But after the 12th century it became the most consistently popular name in Europe, either as the

Mediterranean **Maria**, the French **Marie**, the Welsh **Mair** or the Irish **Moira** and **Maureen**. Together with the many variations, the name is still proving popular today.

MATILDA (Maude, Maud, Maudie, Matty, Mattie, Tilda, Tilly)
Derives from two Old German words meaning 'strength' and 'battle'. These names are not common in modern times, though still appear intermittently.

MAUD(E) see **MATILDA**

MAUREEN (Maurine, Mo)
A modern name, stemming from a diminutive of the Irish **Maire**, a form of **Mary**, which soon spread to the rest of Britain. The name is still quite widespread, particularly in Ireland and Scotland.

MAVIS
An old country name for a 'song thrush', the name was used as a given name in late Victorian times, when 'nature' names were in vogue.

MAXINE (Maxime, Maxeen, Max, Maxie)
A French feminine form of Maximilian meaning 'greatest'. It has been adopted in English-speaking countries during the 20th century, and is now quite widespread.

MAY (Mae, Mai, Maya, Maia)
Derives from the Romans naming their spring month after Maia, their Earth Mother, whom they honoured with festivities on May Day. The name is also a pet form of **Mary**, and sometimes **Margaret**.

MEG see **MARGARET** and **MEGAN**

MEGAN
A Welsh name which developed from **Meg**, one of the pet names of **Margaret** meaning 'pearl'. Its use spread in the early 1900s, and the name has enjoyed considerable popularity ever since.

MELANIE (Melany, Melly, Mellie, Mel)
Derives from the Greek, meaning 'dark-complexioned' or 'black'. Melina was an ancient classical name by which the Greek goddess Demeter was sometimes known. In France **Mèlanie** was quite a common name, and it is believed to have been brought from there by the Huguenots in the 17th century. Recently the name is becoming more popular.

MELINDA (Melly, Melly, Mel)
A combination of Greek and Latin words, meaning 'sweet' and 'soft', which was popular in the 17th century, and now appears to be enjoying something of a revival.

MELISSA (Melisa, Misha, Mellie, Melly, Mel)
Originates from the Greek word meaning 'a bee'. A name with honey-sweet associations, it was used as a personal name 200 years ago, then made a comeback in the middle of the 20th century. It is becoming a top favourite with American parents and is also undergoing something of a revival in Britain.

MELODY (Melodie, Mellie, Melly, Mel)
First used as a girls' name in the late 18th century, meaning just what it says. It is now firmly established and seems to be increasing in popularity.

MERCY
A 'virtue' name, favoured by the Puritans of the 17th century.

MEREDITH (Merry)
Derives from two Old Welsh words, meaning 'great chief'. Originally a surname adapted to a boys' name, given by Welsh parents in the last century. In recent years, as it spread to other countries, it has been used more often for girls.

MERIEL
A Celtic name meaning 'bright as the sea'.

MERLE (Meryl, Merel, Merryl, Merrill)
Originates from the French for 'blackbird'. The name is rare in Britain, but occurs quite frequently in the United States and Canada.

MIA
The Danish pet form of **Mary**, the name has become popular in recent times.

MICHAELA
The feminine form of Michael, meaning 'who is like God', the name has been popular since the 1950s.

MICHELLE (Chelle, Chellie, Shelly, Shelley, Mica, Misha)
The French feminine form of Michael, meaning 'God like', has been in popular use in Britain since the 1960s.

MILDRED (Millie, Milly)
Derives from the Anglo-Saxon name Milthryth, meaning 'gentle power', and was favoured by the Victorians.

MILLICENT (Melisande, Millie, Milly)
Stems from the Old German meaning 'work' or 'strong', the name first came to England in the 12th century, in the French form **Mèlissande**. It was fashionable in Victorian times but is rather unusual now.

MIMI see MARIE

MINA (Minna)
These are pet forms of **Wilhelmina**, but have also often occurred as independent names.

MINNIE
Usually taken to be a Scottish pet form of **Mary**, it is also an abbreviation of **Wilhelmina**, the feminine version of William.

MIRANDA (Mandy)
Means 'worthy to be admired' in Latin, and was coined by Shakespeare for his heroine in *The Tempest*. Parents have taken it up increasingly in recent years.

MIRIAM
Miriam is the earliest form of **Mary** and its meaning is uncertain. The name of an Old Testament prophetess, it only came into use in Britain in the 17th century. It is particularly favoured by Jewish families.

MOIRA (Moyra)
An anglicisation of **Maire**, the Irish form of **Mary**.
It has become a well-liked name in its own right,
especially in Scotland.

MOLLY
An affectionate form of **Mary**, which has long been
recognised as a name in its own right.

MONA
Holds the meaning of 'noble angel' or 'nun'. This
anglicised form of the Irish name Maudhnait came
into vogue in both England and Ireland in the last
century. People who live on the Isle of Man know it
as the Latin name for their island.

MONICA (Monique)
The name of a 4th-century saint, the mother of St
Augustine, who came from North Africa. The origins
and meaning of the name are unknown. It was often
used earlier this century but in the past few years
parents have preferred the French form **Monique**.

MORAG
A Gaelic name meaning 'sun', found mostly in
Scotland. The name is also thought to be a Gaelic
form of **Sarah**.

MORGAN
From the Welsh, meaning 'sea bright'. A surname, now
used as a first name for both girls and boys.

MORNA (Myrna)
An unusual girls' name which comes from the Gaelic
for 'beloved'.

MURIEL
An old Celtic name meaning 'sea'. It was popular in
the Middle Ages, then fell out of use before coming
back into fashion in Victorian times.

MYRA
A name invented by the 16th-century poet Fulke
Greville which proved more popular with writers
than parents, until recent times, when Scottish
parents in particular, have shown a liking for it.

MYRNA see **MORNA**

MYRTLE
Derives from the plant of the same name.

NADIA (Nadine, Nada, Nadya, Nadeem)
The Serbo-Croat form of the Russian name Nadezhda, meaning 'hope'. It is sometimes used in English-speaking countries, though not so frequently as the French form, **Nadine**.

NADINE see **NADIA**

NANCY (Nan)
Originally derives from **Nan**, the pet form for **Anne** and has the same meaning, 'grace'. It has been used as a name in its own right for around 200 years.

NANETTE (Nan)
Another diminutive of **Nan**, the pet form of **Anne**. The name has been used in Britain since the early 20th century.

NAOMI
Hebrew for 'pleasant', this name was a natural Puritan choice with its pleasant meaning, and its biblical association with the long-suffering mother-in-law of Ruth. The name is still considerably popular today.

NARELLE
This charming girls' name is unique; it seems to occur only in Australia, where it is very popular.

NATALIA see **NATALIE**

NATALIE (Natalia, Nathalie, Noel, Noelle)
Derives from the Latin for 'the Lord's birthday'. The
French form **Natalie,** is a well-known name in English-
speaking countries, and has become very popular in
Britain and Australia during the last decade. **Natalia**
is much less common.

NATASHA (Tasha)
The Russian pet form of **Natalie,** which has long been
used as an independent name in English-speaking
countries. It is sometimes shortened to **Tasha.**

NEDA
Possibly Slavonic and means 'Sunday's child'.

NELL (Nelle, Nellie, Nelly)
These are old pet forms of **Eleanor** and **Helen,** but
they have also been used as independent names.

NERISSA
From the Greek, meaning 'sea-nymph'. Shakespeare
seems to have invented the name he gave to Portia's
confidante in the *Merchant of Venice* (1595).

NERYS
A modern Welsh name, meaning 'lady'.

NESSIE see **NESTA**

NESTA (Nessie, Nessa, Ness)
A Welsh name and a pet form of **Agnes,** it was the name
of an 11th-century Welsh princess, and in the 12th century
it was quite well known in Wales. It is sometimes given
as an individual name, but has never been very common.

NICHOLE (Nicole, Nicholette, Nicki, Nickie, Nicky)
The French form of **Nicola**, and especially popular in English-speaking countries at the present time, in keeping with the high esteem in which Nicholas is currently held. On the whole, it is used more in Canada and Australia than in Britain, where **Nicola** is preferred.

NICOLA (Nichola, Nicolina, Nicki, Nickie, Nicky, Nick)
The feminine form of Nicholas, meaning 'the peoples' triumph', has been far more popular than the boys' name, becoming one of the most fashionable names for girls over the past few years.

NINA (Ninette)
Began as a pet form for the Russian **Annina** or the French Nanine, both versions of Anne, meaning 'grace'. It has been used as an independent name over the past 100 years, and is quite a well-known name in English-speaking countries, though not particularly common.

NITA
A pet form of the Spanish name Juanita, now generally used.

NOELLE (Noel, Noeleen)
Derives from the French for 'Christmas', and since the Middle Ages has been used as a name for both boys and girls, born at this time of year. Nowadays the feminine form is usually **Noelle**.

NORA (Norah, Noreen)
Originally an Irish diminutive of the name **Honora**, meaning 'honour', it has been accepted as an independent name since the Midle Ages. It was popular with Irish parents long before it found favour with the English at the end of the 19th century. See also **Eleanor**.

NOREEN see NORA

NORMA
Possibly from the Latin, meaning 'rule', but this is by no means certain. It could simply be the feminine form of Norman. It did not become widespread until the 1920s, when it was quite popular for a time both in Britain and the United States.

NUALA
From the Irish name Fionnhuala, meaning 'white-shouldered'. Legend has it that the beautiful Fionnhuala was transformed into a swan by her evil stepmother, wandering the lakes and rivers endlessly. She could not be released from the spell until Christianity came to Ireland.

NYREE
A Maori word of unknown meaning. It was introduced to Britain by actress Nyree Dawn Porter.

OCTAVIA
Derives from Latin and means 'eighth girl'. It is normally used independent of its meaning.

ODETTE
The French feminine of an Old German name meaning 'rich'. Used as a given name in Britain during the 20th century and made famous by the 1950 film of the same name, based on the true story of a wartime resistance heroine. It is still however, an uncommon name in Britain.

OENONE
A nymph featuring in Greek mythology, possessing the gifts of prophecy and healing.

OLGA
This Russian name derives from Helga, an Old Norse name meaning 'holy'. It came to Britain during the 19th century.

OLIVE (Olivia, Ollie, Livia, Livvy, Liv, Nollie)
Derives from the Latin *oliva* meaning 'olive', and is the ancient symbol of peace. The name is first recorded in the 13th century in the form Oliva. By the 17th century **Olive** was firmly established as a first name, and the Italian version **Olivia** was taken up in the 18th century, a period when Italian names were fashionable. Both forms survived and have been well-represented in the 20th century.

OLIVIA see **OLIVE**

OLWEN (Olwin, Ollie)

From the Welsh, meaning 'white footprint'. Olwen was a giant's daughter in Welsh mythology; as she walked, white flowers appeared beneath her feet.

OLYMPIA

An ancient Greek name meaning 'heavenly one'. Nowadays its immediate connection is with the Olympic Games.

OPHELIA

With the meaning of 'help', this was a name popular with Victorians, more for its medieval origins than for the fate of the beautiful heroine in Shakespeare's *Hamlet*.

ORIEL

Possibly a variation of Auriel, meaning 'golden', the name was, however, brought to Britain with the Norman Conquest.

OTTILIE (Ottilia)

From the Old German, meaning 'fatherland', the feminine version of Otto.

PAIGE

An occupational surname, meaning 'page'; now a modern first name for girls, especially popular in the United States.

PAINTON

The name of a country town introduced by the Normans, but only used occasionally today.

PALOMA (Paolma)

Holds the meaning of a 'dove', like the olive, a symbol of peace. The painter Picasso gave this Spanish name to his daughter.

PAMELA

Pamela stems from two Greek words meaning 'all honey', and was first used as a Christian name in the works of Sir Philip Sidney, in the 16th century. It was at its most fashionable around the middle of the 20th century and is often shortened to **Pam** or **Pammie**.

PANDORA

Means 'multi-gifted'. In Greek mythology each god gave Pandora a power to bring about the downfall of man. When her husband opened Jupiter's present, a box, the evils of the world flew out.

PASCALE

The French name refers to the Passover, or to Easter, so it is apt for an Easter baby.

PAT see **PATRICIA**

PATIENCE (Patty)
An abstract 'virtue' name, it came into use in the
17th century, occasionally also given to a boy. Unlike
many others of the same kind, this name survived and
continues in regular use up to the present day.

PATRICE
The French form of **Patricia**, sometimes used as an
alternative version in English-speaking countries.

PATRICIA (Pat, Patty, Patti, Patsy, Trish, Tricia)
The feminine form of Patrick, meaning 'aristocrat'. It
became popular at the end of the 19th century through
Queen Victoria's granddaughter, Princess Patricia of
Connaught, and is still quite common.

PATSY
A short form of **Patricia**, sometimes treated as an
independent name during the 20th century.

PATTY (Patti) see **PATIENCE** and **PATRICIA**

PAULA
A feminine form of Paul which is derived from the
Latin and means 'small'. Never in use to any extent
until the 20th century.

PAULINE (Paulina, Pauleen, Paulette)
Pauline is the French, and most often used feminine
form of Paul in English-speaking countries, though
it has never been used as often as its popular male
equivalent.

PEARL (Pearle, Pearla)
One of the jewel names in vogue in Victorian times which has survived to the present day.

PEGGY (Peggie, Peg)
One of the many pet forms of **Margaret** which has come to be regarded as an independent name.

PENELOPE (Penny, Pen)
From the Greek meaning 'weaver'. In Greek mythology Odysseus returned from travelling to find his faithful wife Penelope, had craftily repelled her suitors. She promised to select one when she had finished her weaving, but secretly unpicked her day's work each night.

PENNY
A shortened form of **Penelope**, sometimes regarded as an individual name in its own right.

PERDITA (Purdie)
Derives from the Latin, meaning 'lost'. Perdita, the heroine of Shakespeare's play, *The Winter's Tale*, is abandoned on a deserted shore and raised by a shepherd, even though really she is a princess. Shakespeare appears to have invented the name.

PERSEPHONE
From the Greek, meaning 'dazzlingly bright'.

PETULA (Petra)
Derives from the Latin meaning 'seeker', but with **Petra**, is sometimes looked on as a feminine form of Peter.

PETRONELLA
The name of an early Christian martyr, it has been used in England since the 12th century. Medieval legend has it that Petronella was the daughter of the apostle Peter, being invoked by those suffering from fever.

PHILIPPA (Phil, Pip, Pippa)
Originates from the Greek, meaning 'lover of horses', and is the female equivalent of Philip. Philippa remained in regular use throughout the 19th and 20th centuries, though it has never been widely used.

PHILOMENA
An unusual girls' name that derives from the Greek for 'nightingale', sometimes given as 'lover of the moon'. **Phil** is the short form.

PHOEBE (Phebe, Pheby)
Means 'the shining one', and was one of the names given by the ancient Greeks to the moon goddess. It caught the imagination of Victorian parents and is still used today.

PHYLLIS (Phillida, Phil)
Has the meaning of 'leafy', coming from the name of a maiden in Greek mythology who turned into a tree, after she had killed herself for love.

PIA
Meaning 'dutiful', this name, implying piousness and faithfulness, is now gaining popularity.

PIPPA
A pet form of **Philippa**, regarded as an independent name.

PLEASANCE
From the Old French, meaning 'to please'. This was
brought to England by the Normans.

POLLY
A rhyming variation of **Molly,** a short form of both
Margaret and **Mary.** Used independently since the
18th century, when John Gay chose it for the heroine
of *The Beggar's Opera* (1727).

POPPY
A Victorian flower name now enjoying a revival.

PORTIA
A Latin name meaning 'an offering to God'. It was
made popular by Shakespeare's *Merchant of Venice*.

PRIMROSE
An 'early rose'. The delicate, pale yellow blossoms
made this a particularly popular Victorian flower name,
introduced at the end of the 19th century.

PRIMULA
A botanical name, used as a first name since the late
19th century.

PRISCILLA (Cilla, Precilla)
Derives from the Latin word for 'ancient'. It was in
vogue with the 18th-century Puritans and again with
the Victorians, remaining in general use, though it is
no longer very common.

PRUDENCE (Prue, Pru)
One of the most popular of the abstract 'virtue' names which were so much in vogue after the Reformation, and in the 17th century. Unlike similar names, this one is still in regular use.

PRUNELLA (Prue, Pru)
Originates from the Latin, meaning 'little plum'. Unfortunately this is all that seems to be known about this rather charming name.

Q

QUEENIE
The name implies 'a supreme woman', whether she is queen of a man's heart, a house or a realm. Used as an affectionate first name for Queen Victoria, and then by the Edwardians.

QUINTA (Quintana)
From the Latin, meaning 'fifth'. The feminine form of Quintin and much used in Ancient Rome. **Quintana** is a modern variation.

R

RACHEL (Rachelle, Rae, Ray)
From the Hebrew meaning 'ewe'. A biblical name given
to Jacob's wife, and symbolising innocence. This Old
Testament name, which has always been a favourite
with the Jewish people, came to England after the
Reformation and has been in constant use since the
17th century. In the last decade it has been especially
successful in all English-speaking countries, and is still
extremely popular.

RAE see **RACHEL**

RAMONA
The feminine form of Ramon, the Spanish version of
Raymond meaning 'wise guardian'.

RANA
A name of Asian origin meaning 'a queen of birth'.

RAPHAELA
Stems from Hebrew and means 'healed by God'.

REBECCA (Rebekah, Becca, Beckie, Becky)
A Hebrew name of uncertain origin, possibly meaning
'a knotted cord'. The name of Isaac's beautiful wife in
the Old Testament implies faithfulness, and the name
has been consistently used throughout time.

REGINA (Reina, Reine, Rena, Gina)
Derives from the Latin meaning 'queen'. Both **Regina**
and **Reina,** the English version of the French **Reine,**
occurred in the 13th century. The name largely went

out of use in Britain (though it was still well known in Europe) until the 19th century, when it had a brief revival. Since then it has again become rare in Britain, but occurs more frequently in the United States.

RENA see REGINA

RENÈE (Renata, Renate)
A French name derived from the Latin, meaning 'born again'. It is quite popular in some English-speaking countries, and has recently become a favourite in Australia.

RHIAN
From the Welsh, meaning 'maiden'. A modern name.

RHIANNON
From the Welsh, meaning 'nymph' or 'goddess'.

RHODA
This Roman name referred to Rhodes, island of roses. Popular during the 19th century, and recently revived.

RHONA
A name of uncertain origin; possibily stemming from a contraction of **Rowena**, or a Scottish place name. It first appeared about 100 years ago and has been used, on the whole, by Scottish parents.

RHONDA
Rhonda is a place name in Wales that has also been used as a girls' name, particularly in the United States.

RICHENDA
An 18th century feminine form of Richard, meaning 'powerful ruler'. The name is very rare today.

RILLA
From the German, meaning 'brook'.

RITA
This is really an abbreviation of **Margherita**, the Italian form of **Margaret**, but has long been recognised as an independent name, accepted in English-speaking countries as one of their own.

ROBERTA (Bobby, Robin, Robina, Robyn, Ruby)
The feminine form of Robert, meaning 'illustrious' or 'fame'.

ROBIN (Robyn, Robina)
Originally another version of Rob, the diminutive of Robert, but has been established as an independent name for several hundred years. The first feminine form was **Robina** but **Robin** or **Robyn** is now used for girls as well as boys.

ROMAINE (Romayne)
A French feminine name, meaning 'Roman', now generally used.

RONA (Rhona)
One of those interesting names whose origins are open to wide-ranging suggestions. It is possibly a contraction of **Rowena**, a variant spelling of **Rhonda**, or as suggested by one authority, the name taken from the Gaelic word for 'a seal'.

ROSA see **ROSE**

ROSALIE (Rosalia)
Derives from a Latin word meaning 'rose'. The older
version is **Rosalia**, but the French form **Rosalie** has
been more successful with modern parents.

**ROSALIND (Rosaline, Rosalinda, Rosaleen,
Rosalyn, Ros)**
Originally Old German, *roslindis*, meaning 'horse
and serpent', but when the name reached Spain as
Rosalinda it took the Spanish meaning of 'rose', and
'pretty' from the Spanish word *linda*, a much more
acceptable interpretation.

ROSAMOND (Rosamund, Ros)
Rosamund originally derives from Old German
meaning 'horse protector'. However, in the Middle
Ages scholars decided that it was from Latin, with
the more attractive meaning 'rose of the world'. A
modern spelling is **Rosamond** which is still in
general use, though not very common.

ROSANNE see **ROSE**

ROSE (Rosa, Rosanne, Rosanna)
Originally from the German *hros*, 'horse', an animal
revered by the early Germanic people. It is with the
flower, however, that the name is usually associated.
The Normans introduced **Rose** to England as Roese
and Rohese, and it also appeared in other forms
before becoming established.

194

ROSEMARY (Rosemarie)

Derives from the Latin meaning 'dew of the sea'. The Christian name is believed to have been first devised from the combination of **Rose** with **Mary** in the 18th century.

ROSLYN (Rosslyn, Roslynn, Roslin)

A Scottish place name used as a girls' name. Some of its variations, such as **Rosalyn**, suggest it is closely associated with **Rosalind**.

ROWAN (Rowena, Rohnwen)

This anglicised form of the Welsh name meaning 'slender' is becoming increasingly popular. The name can also be linked with the rowan tree, which was believed to have the power to drive away evil.

ROXANA (Roxanna, Roxane, Roxanne, Roxy)

Derives from the Persian word for 'dawn', and was the heroine of a novel of that name by Daniel Defoe.

RUBY

A 'gem' name, first used by the Victorians in the late 19th century. Fine quality rubies are the costliest of all gems.

RUTH

The origin is uncertain, probably Hebrew, meaning either 'version of beauty' or 'friend'. This is a biblical favourite, brought into use by the Puritans in the 17th century and remaining in regular use ever since.

S

SABINA (Sabin, Sabine)
Stems from the Latin meaning 'from the Sabine region'. It has been used as a personal name in Britain for 300 years, though it has never been particularly common.

SABRINA (Brina, Brie)
Derives from a poetic Roman name for the river Severn, though the original meaning is not known. In recent years it has been used more often in the United States than Britain, and can be shortened to **Brina** or **Brie**.

SACHA
From the Greek, meaning 'helper of mankind'. It is used both as a boys' and a girls' name.

SADIE
A pet form of **Sarah**, used as an independent name since the late 19th century.

SAFFRON
A modern name, taken from the flower or spice; saffron being the most expensive spice in the world.

SALLY (Sallie, Sal)
Originally used as a pet name for **Sarah**, meaning 'princess', but has been established as a name in its own right for 200 years.

SALLYANN
There has been a move towards some of these 'combination' names in recent years. This is one which is gaining favour.

SAMANTHA (Sammie, Sammy, Sam)
Thought to mean 'heard', a name implying the granting of parents' prayers for a child. It has had a meteoric rise in popularity and it is now in the top 50 names of most English-speaking countries, though not in the United States, where it has never been quite such a success.

SANDRA (Sandie, Sandy, Zandra)
A fairly modern name which began as a diminutive of the Italian name **Alessandra**, itself a version of **Alexandra**. The original meaning was 'defender of men'.

SANDY see **SANDRA**

SARAH (Sara, Sadie, Sallie, Sally, Sarai, Sarena, Sarra, Zara, Zoreen)
Stems from the Hebrew meaning 'princess', and was the name of Abraham's wife in the Old Testament. It was very popular for 300 years, until it went out of vogue at the turn of the century, only to make a great comeback as one of today's favourites.

SASKIA
A Dutch name, popular in Britain for the last 20 years.

SCARLETT (Scarlette)
Originally a Middle English word meaning 'colour of scarlet', probably a cloth trader's surname turned first name. However, it came immediately to the fore, due to the heroine of the novel *Gone with the Wind* - Scarlett O'Hara.

SELINA
Can be linked with the moon. The golden crown of the Greek goddess of the moon, also known as **Artemisia** and **Phoebe**, illuminated the skies, as she crossed them nightly.

SERENA
Thought to mean 'calm' and 'clear'. This name was popular with early Christians in Rome, arriving in Britain in the 18th century.

SHANNON
Derives from Gaelic and means 'old wise one', also being the name of an Irish river.

SHARON (Sharen, Sharron, Sharan, Sharene, Shari, Shara)
Meaning 'the plain' in Hebrew, this name appears as a place name in the Bible. When first used, in the 17th century, it was a boys' name but when it came into fashion in the middle of the 20th century, it was used only for girls.

SHEENA (Shena, Sheona, Sheenah, Sheenagh)
The English pronunciation of the name Sine, which is the Gaelic for **Jane**, meaning 'God is gracious'.

SHEILA (Sheela, Sheelah, Sheelagh, Shelly)
Originates from the English pronunciation of the Irish
name Sile, a form of **Celia**, meaning 'heavenly'. Its Irish
origins were forgotten when it became popular all over
Britain in the first half of the 20th century.

SHELLEY (Shelly)
Stems from an Old English place name, meaning
'clearing on a slope' which became first a surname,
then a personal name for boys. During the 20th century
it has become well known as a girls' name.

**SHEREE (Sherry, Sheri, Sherri, Sherrie, Cherie,
Cherrie)**
The English version of the French word *chèrie*, meaning
'darling'.

SHERYL (Sherryl) see **SHIRLEY**

SHIRLEY (Sheryl, Sherryl, Sherill, Shirl)
A surname which developed from an English place
name meaning 'bright meadow'. Novelist Charlotte
Brontë first used it as a girls' name for her heroine
in *Shirley* (1849), and it has been very successful
ever since.

SHONA
An anglicised form of the Gaelic name Seonaid, the
female form of Shaun, meaning 'God's mercy'.

SIAN
The Welsh form of **Jane**, now generally used.

SIBYL (Sybil, Sibel, Sibilla, Sibylla, Sibbie)
Derives from Ancient Greece and Rome, where it denoted the collective name of the guardians of the sibylline oracles.

SIENA
Deriving from the Italian city, this has been used as a first name since the 19th century.

SILVIA see **SYLVIA**

SIMONE (Simona)
The feminine form of Simon, meaning 'snub nosed'. This is a name which has been better known in France than in English-speaking countries. However, since the 1970s, it has been an unprecedented success in Australia.

SINEAD
The Gaelic form of **Janet**, now increasing in popularity generally.

SIOBHAN (Shavon, Shevon)
The Irish form of **Joan**, meaning 'grace of God'. A favourite girls' name in Ireland, and to a lesser extent, Scotland.

SONIA (Sonja, Sonya)
Originally a Russian pet form of **Sophia**, adopted by English-speaking parents during the 19th century to become considerably popular.

SOPHIA

Originating from the Greek, meaning 'wisdom', this was essentially an aristocratic name. It was a favourite in European royal circles, and came into use in England following the Hanoverian succession.

SOPHIE

The modern French form of **Sophia**, from the Greek meaning 'wisdom'. This is now firmly established as a separate name, and has become extremely popular.

SOROYA

A Persian name meaning 'seven stars'.

STACEY (Stacy, Stacie, Stacia)

Probably started life as a pet form of **Eustacia** or **Anastasia**, meaning 'she will rise again', but has become popular as an independent name in its own right, taking its place among the 'new' names of the 1970s.

STELLA (Estella, Estelle)

The Latin for 'star'. The name was almost unknown before the 16th-century poet, Sir Philip Sidney, made it famous in his sonnets. Parents, however, only began using it in large numbers at the beginning of the 20th century.

STEPHANIE (Stephania, Stefanie, Steffi, Steph)

This French female form of Stephen, meaning 'crown' and used by early Christians as **Stephania**, came to Britain in the 1920s. It has benefited from the rise in popularity of Stephen in the last two decades, and is now fairly widespread.

SUSAN (Suzanne, Susanne, Susannah, Suzanna, Suzette, Suky, Susie, Suzie, Suzy, Sue)
Derives from the Hebrew for 'lily', and in the older form, **Susannah**, is a biblical name, used in Britain since the 13th century. In modern times, **Susan** took over to become one of the most widely used girls' names in the English-speaking world. French forms are **Suzanne** and **Susanne**, and recently, seem to be preferred.

SUSANNE (Suzanne) see SUSAN

SUSIE (Suzie, Suzy) see SUSAN

SUZETTE see SUSAN

SYBIL see SIBYL

SYLVIA (Silvia, Sylvie)
Derives from the Latin word for 'wood'. In the 17th and 19th centuries the name was used mainly by poets, then parents took it up and made it popular in the first half of the 20th century.

SYRIE
A feminine form of Cyril, from the Greek meaning 'lord'. The name is now enjoying a revival.

T

TABITHA
Derives from Hebrew and means 'gazelle'. It became popular in recent times, due to the success of the TV series *Bewitched*.

TALLULAH
From the American Indian place name, meaning 'running water'. Tallulah Falls is a notable beauty spot in the American state of Georgia.

TAMARA (Tammy)
Originates from Hebrew and means 'palm tree'. It has been growing in popularity in recent times.

TAMSIN (Tamsyn, Tamasin, Tamsine, Tammy)
An old Cornish form of Thomasina, the feminine form of Thomas, meaning 'twin'. It has recently entered the lists of modern names and is doing very nicely, especially in its pet form, **Tammy**.

TANIA (Tanya)
A shortening of the Russian name **Tatiana**, though its meaning is unknown. It has been frequently used in Britain as an independent name over the past 20 years.

TANSY
From the flower, derived from the Greek *athanasia*, meaning 'immortality'. It became popular as a first name in the 20th century.

TARA
An Irish place name, the ancient coronation site of the Irish kings. This is another of the 'new' names which has swung into popularity in the last decade, especially in the United States and Canada.

TASSA see TERESA

TATIANA (Tania, Tanya)
A Russian name, used as a first name in Britain since the early 20th century, however, not as popular as its derivatives.

TATUM
This female form of Tate has the meaning of 'spirited'.

TERESA (Terese, Theresa, Tessa, Tessie, Tess, Terry, Terri, Tracey, Tracy)
Of unknown origin, but may stem from the Greek word, meaning 'to reap'. It began as a Spanish name, spreading among Roman Catholic families all over the world, with the fame of St Teresa of Avila in the 16th century. As a predominantly Roman Catholic name, has always been highly thought of in Ireland, and recently its success rating has been climbing in the rest of Britain too.

TESSA (Tess)
Originally Old English pet names for **Teresa**, these have long been used as names in their own right, with their own diminutive **Tessie**.

TERRI (Terry) see TERESA

THALIA (Talia)
In Greek mythology one of the nine Muses, daughter
of Zeus and Mnemosyne. Thalia is the muse of comedy,
represented in art as holding a comic mask and a
shepherd's crook.

THEA
Meaning 'goddess', this Greek name, now fully
independent, was originally a short form of **Dorothea**
and **Theodora**.

THELMA
Invented by the novelist Marie Corelli in 1887, this
name caught the public eye at once and soon became
widespread. It still occurs fairly frequently.

THEODORA (Fedora, Thandine)
First used by early Christians in Rome, this female
form of Theodore meaning 'gift of God', is currently
more popular than its reversed form, **Dorothea**.

THERESA see **TERESA**

THORA
Originates from Thor, the Norse god of thunder and
war, after whom Thursday, Thor's day is named.

TIFFANY (Tiff)
Originally the short form of the vanished name
Theophinia, from the Greek meaning, 'manifestation
of God', and given to girls born at Epiphany. Tiffany
has undergone a revival recently.

TILLY (Tillie) see **MATILDA**

TINA
Originally this was simply a pet form of names which ended with 'tina', such as **Christina**, but it has since come to be regarded as a name in its own right.

TONI
An abbreviated form of **Antonia**, and used as a girls' name in its own right. The spelling distinguishes it from the boys' name Tony.

TONIA (Tonya)
A short form of **Antoinette** which is now recognised as an individual name.

TRACEY (Tracy, Trasey)
Believed to be a form of **Teresa**, this has been a highly successful girls' name in recent years, in most of the English-speaking countries.

TOYAH
An Old English word, meaning 'whimsical' or 'sporty', that has only recently been given as a first name.

TRIXIE see BEATRICE

TRUDY (Trudie, Trudi)
Originally a pet form of **Gertrude** and **Ermintrude**, both of which have faded out of modern use. It is now a well-established independent name.

TUESDAY
The day of the week, only recently adopted as a first name, honours the Teutonic god of war.

U

UNA (Oonagh)

Una is the English spelling of the ancient Irish name **Oonagh** and its meaning is uncertain; it may be linked with the Latin for 'one' or the Irish for 'lamb'. It has been used outside Ireland for over a century now, though still remains fairly unusual.

UNITY

An abstract 'virtue' name which was brought into use by the Puritans in the 17th century. Though it has occasionally appeared in the 20th century, it is now rare.

URSULA (Ursa, Ursel, Ursella, Ursie)

Derives from the Latin, meaning 'she-bear' and was made famous by the 5th-century saint, martyred along with 11,000 virgins. It was popular in medieval times, then again in the 17th century and has survived the generations, though it is no longer very common.

V

VALENTINE (Valentina)

A name for both sexes, honouring the Roman saint martyred on February 13, the eve of the pagan festival for lovers. He was later remembered on the festival day, 'St Valentines's day', with its traditions.

VALERIE (Valeria, Valery, Val)

Originally the feminine form of a famous Roman family name, probably meaning 'to be in good health'. It was used in Victorian times as **Valeria**, but **Valerie**, coming to England from France, soon took over. It was very successful in the first half of the 20th century, and is still used regularly.

VANESSA (Nessa, Nessie, Ness, Vanni)

A form of **Esther**, invented by Jonathan Swift to disguise Esther Vanhomrigh's name when he recounted their love affair in his poem *Cadenus and Vanessa* (1713). Parents were slow to take it up as a personal name, but it has been used quite often since the 1950s.

VELMA see WILHEMINA

VENITIA

The Latin form of the city of Venice, used as a first name since the 16th century, although never particularly well-known.

VERA

Derives from the Russian word for 'faith' and came into use in late Victorian times. It made its greatest impact in the first half of the 20th century.

VERITY (Verita)
Originates from the Latin for 'truth', being one of the many 'virtue' names given to girls by the 17th-century Puritans. It has remained in use ever since, but has never been common.

VERONICA (Véronique, Ronnie, Ron)
Derives from the Latin for 'true image'; it was the name given to the woman who wiped the face of Jesus with a cloth, which retained the image of his face. As **Vèronique** it was a popular name in France long before it reached Scotland in the 17th century, only spreading to England during the past 100 years.

VICKI (Vicky, Vickie, Vikki)
Meaning 'conqueror', this short form of **Victoria** is now fully independent, and a top favourite choice.

VICTORIA (Victorie, Victorine, Vicky)
The Latin word for 'victory' was hardly ever used as a given name in Britain before Queen Victoria's accession to the throne. Even then it was normally used as a second name, only becoming a favourite in recent years.

VIOLA see **VIOLET**

VIOLET (Viola, Violette, Violetta)
One of the oldest of the flower names, Violet is a flower name symbolising modesty. **Viola,** the older Latin form, as used by Shakespeare in *Twelfth Night*, has completely given way to the English form Violet, which came into its own with the fashion for flower names towards the end of the 19th century. It was popular during the first quarter of the 20th century and is still in general use.

209

VIRGINIA (Ginnie, Ginny, Jinny)
Originates from an ancient Roman clan name, probably meaning 'manly race', and has been used as a first name in England for nearly 200 years. In the United States it has different origins: parents took the name from the state of Virginia, which in turn was named after Queen Elizabeth I, the Virgin Queen.

VITA
A name meaning 'life', popularised this century by the novelist Vita Sackville-West, who created the gardens of Sissinghurst Castle.

VIVIEN (Vivienne, Vivian, Vivianne, Viviana, Viv)
Derives from the Latin word meaning 'alive'. **Vivian**, the usual spelling for a boys' name, dates from medieval times, but is seldom used today. The feminine form Vivien has been successful this century, making its biggest impact, with the French spelling **Vivienne**, in the 1950s.

WALLACE (Wallis)
A name for boys and girls, derived from an Anglo-Saxon word meaning 'foreign'. Used as a surname in Scotland, it was first used as a first name in the 19th century, but has never become widespread. **Wallis** is an alternative spelling sometimes used for girls.

WANDA
Has Germanic roots but its meaning is uncertain; some suggestions are 'kindred' and 'stock'. The name is more common in the United States, only now gaining popularity in Britain.

WENDY (Wendie, Wenda)
A name invented by playwright J.M. Barrie for the heroine of *Peter Pan* (1904). Parents took it up a few years later, and it has since enjoyed a career of unbroken success.

WILLA
A pet form of the German name **Wilhelmina**, now used independently.

WILHELMINA (Williamina, Willa, Velma, Vilma, Mina, Minna)
The feminine form of Wilhelm, the German version of William, meaning 'resolute guardian'. The name is occasionally borrowed in English-speaking countries, and is especially liked in Scotland.

WINIFRED (Wyn, Winnie, Freddy, Freda)
A Welsh name meaning 'blessed reconciliation'. This was the name of a saint, at whose shrine there is a miraculous well. It has remained in general use but is not common today.

WYNN
From the Welsh, meaning 'fair'. Used as a first name since the mid-20th century.

X

XANTHE
The name of the hero Achilles' horse. A girls' name posessing the meaning 'yellow', making it a suitable name for a fair child.

XENIA (Xena, Zenia, Zena)
A girls' name, taken from the Greek for 'guest'. **Zenia** is an alternative spelling which indicates the pronunciation.

YASMINE
Deriving from Arabic, this 'flower' name is an Asian, softer-sounding, form of the English name **Jasmine**.

YOKO
Has the meaning of 'a determined woman', this name was largely made famous in the West by Yoko Ono, who married Beatle John Lennon.

YOLANDE (Yolanda)
A medieval French name, from the Greek meaning 'violet flower', which is a variation on the diminutive form of **Viola**. **Yolanda** is quite well known in the United States and Canada, but neither form of the name is common in Britain.

YVETTE
A French feminine form of the boys' name, Yves. It is a very common name in France, and is occasionally used in English-speaking countries, though it is fairly rare in Britain.

YVONNE
Another French feminine form of the boys' name, Yves. Although this has exactly the same background as **Yvette**, for some reason it has been much more easily assimilated to English name usage, and is now thought of as an English rather than a French name.

Z

ZARA (Zaira)
Originates from an Arabic word meaning 'splendour of the east'. It received a boost when the Princess Royal used it at her daughter's christening in 1981.

ZELDA
This is really the end part of the name **Grizelda**, treated as an independent name.

ZELLIE
A French name, meaning 'ardent', now generally used.

ZENIA (Zena) see **XENIA**

ZILLAH
From the Hebrew, meaning 'shadow'. The name came into use in England after the Reformation, when non-biblical names were abandoned.

ZILPAH (Zilpha)
From the Hebrew, meaning 'sprinkling'.

ZITA (Zeta)
Believed to be simply the end part of the Spanish name 'Rosita'. This abbreviated form has now become popular, especially in Australia.

ZOE (Zowey, Zoey)
Derives from the Greek for 'life'. It was equated with **Eve** as the 'mother of life'. It was hardly known in England until the 19th century. Since the early 1970s it has become increasingly popular.